NON-TRIAL ADVOCACY

A Case Study Approach

Cavendish
Publishing
Limited

London • Sydney

NON-TRIAL ADVOCACY

A Case Study Approach

Stephen Nathanson, B Comm, LLB
Associate Professor
University of Hong Kong

Cavendish
Publishing
Limited

London • Sydney

First published in Great Britain 2001 by Cavendish Publishing Limited,
The Glass House, Wharton Street, London WC1X 9PX, United Kingdom
Telephone: + 44 (0)20 7278 8000   Facsimile: + 44 (0)20 7278 8080
Email: info@cavendishpublishing.com
Website: www.cavendishpublishing.com

British Library Cataloguing in Publication Data

Nathanson, Stephen
Non-trial advocacy: a case study approach
1 Practice of law – England   2 Practice of law – Wales
I Title
347.4'2'052

ISBN 1 85941 612 8

Printed and bound in Great Britain

PREFACE

Think before you speak.

Few would disagree that, if we all paid a little more attention to this maxim, the world would be a better place. And, every lawyer would agree that thinking before speaking is the most basic rule of the courtroom. But, how do lawyers think when they are thinking about going into court to argue a case? How do they put those thought processes into action and words?

One of the most worthwhile learning experiences for any new lawyer is to be involved in a court case with a team of good lawyers who think out loud, who 'talk strategy'. When well trained legal minds are engaged in strategic advocacy, they are operating at the peak of their intellectual powers. The new lawyer listens as they brainstorm, trying to come up with the best strategy for winning. The new lawyer watches as they focus on the evidence looking for ways to tell their client's story so that it appeals logically and emotionally to the court. The new lawyer helps as they all work ceaselessly, gathering information, organising it and rehearsing. Then, when they all get into court, the new lawyer is impressed by how deftly they implement strategy and how, just as deftly – when the situation calls for it – they suddenly change direction and rethink everything.

Nothing can replace the experience of learning to practise law in this way. This is learning by observing which, along with learning by doing, is one of the cornerstones of professional education. Ideally, however, learning by observing should be supplemented with learning that is more systematic and reflective. Good lawyers are in a hurry and work fast. To the newcomer, their decisions are unpredictable. And, once decisions are made, the experts do not have time to second guess and analyse them. They rarely have time to explain things to their juniors. In using a case study approach to writing this book, I wanted to give readers the sensation that they were among good lawyers working on challenging problems, but that they were being guided through them slowly and systematically with plenty of opportunity for analysis and reflection.

For helping me with this book, I would like to express my gratitude to the Committee on Research and Conference Grants for their financial support and to Vandana Rajwani for her research, her numerous suggestions and the light she shed on many of the theoretical and practical issues raised by the case studies.

I owe a debt of gratitude to Brian Baillee of Adelaide, Australia. Two of the criminal case studies in this book are derived from material he provided.

I am grateful to Gary Blasi who read chapters in draft, made several helpful suggestions and provided critical insights. To Penelope Wacks and Art McInnis I am also indebted for reading chapters and giving me their feedback.

I would like to express my heartfelt gratitude to Ginger Chang who contributed many creative ideas and worked very hard to improve the organisation of material and the quality of the writing.

Stephen Nathanson
2001

CONTENTS

INTRODUCTION

When I first started working as a lawyer in court, I had to learn a lot in a hurry. I had to learn how to listen and speak to people, how to do research, and how to identify and solve problems for clients who put their trust in me. One of the things I remember being most impressed with was how persuasive many of my opponents were in court. In fact, they were often so persuasive, I was sometimes convinced my case had little merit.

Fortunately, after an appropriate period of on-the-job training, I overcame feelings of self-doubt. Through experience, I learned how to investigate the facts, sift through large amounts of information and, ultimately, identify the weaknesses in my opponent's case and the strengths of my own.

The tendency to see only the strengths of other people's arguments is a common one among new lawyers. As an advocacy teacher, I see it in my students. They often say: 'I can't argue these facts. My case is hopeless,' or 'I totally agree with the other side'. Some might think these students do not have the right attitude to be advocates, that they have chosen the wrong profession. But, for an advocate, the ability to see the other party's point of view is essential. It is just that one should not go overboard and be completely persuaded by it.

One of the points stressed in this book is that to argue a case effectively, you have to be able to put yourself in other people's shoes, not only those of the judge, but those of the other side. You cannot put your head in the sand and ignore the other side's argument. You need to anticipate their argument, show you understand it, and help the judge to see that, despite its merits, your case is stronger.

My purpose in writing this book is to help lawyers, particularly new ones, learn to do this by acquiring advocacy skills. The context I am using is non-trial, rather than trial, advocacy. I believe this is a neglected area in the literature on advocacy and, in any event, should be learned before trial advocacy. Most lawyers need to do considerably more non-trial than trial advocacy in their first few years of practice. In fact, it is fair to say that most lawyers probably do more non-trial advocacy than trial advocacy in their careers. Non-trial advocacy skills are easier to learn than trial advocacy skills, and yet are closely related to them.

This book teaches the strategies and techniques of non-trial advocacy through realistic case studies. Each case study includes the facts of the case and, where necessary, supporting documents. Then, the lawyers involved in the case discuss how they are going to deal with it in court. This is followed by transcripts of their oral submissions. The judge then makes an order. Finally, the section entitled *commentary* analyses the strategic decisions taken by the lawyers as well as the techniques they use in court.

NON-TRIAL ADVOCACY

Non-trial advocacy is the advocacy skills that lawyers use in court in pre-trial and post-trial submissions, but not in a trial or an appeal. This book focuses on two kinds of non-trial advocacy skills – those used in criminal cases, such as bail applications and pleas in mitigation, and those used in contested pre-trial applications made in civil actions.

A major distinction between non-trial and trial advocacy is that in non-trial advocacy, witnesses are not called to testify, so there are no opportunities to test the evidence through cross-examination. Since witnesses are not called to the box, lawyers must make their arguments based on evidence from other sources. In bail applications and pleas in mitigation, the prosecution obtains evidence from the police in the form of witness statements or reports of interviews. The defence obtains evidence from the client's instructions, notes of interviews with other witnesses and sometimes witness statements, pre-sentence reports and written testimonials.

In civil applications, evidence is usually in the form of affidavits, which are written statements sworn by a witness in front of a commissioner (usually a solicitor), or written witness statements signed by the witness who states they are true. In making its decision, the court can refer only to these or other documents already filed in the proceedings.

Because there is no witness handling, non-trial hearings are much shorter than trials. Trials are usually measured in days, weeks and months. Non-trial hearings are usually measured in minutes, or hours.

THE CASE STUDY APPROACH

In using a case study approach to teach advocacy, I want to give readers the sense that they are involved in cases as observer-learners with a window on what the lawyers are thinking and how their strategies are translated into courtroom action. This will enable readers to examine at close range the complexity of realistic legal problems and to deepen their understanding of the thought and skill that goes into each legal argument. With most of the case studies, readers will also have the opportunity to learn how advocacy issues are connected to the client's problem as a whole. They will be able to see that advocacy is not just an isolated performance: the lawyer's strategies and techniques for arguing a case in court need to be consistent with the client's goals as well as the lawyer's overall strategy for solving the client's problem.

Readers may not always agree with how the lawyers in this book handle their cases or with the commentary on their performances. But reading and analysing the case studies and related material should provide considerable guidance on how to approach advocacy problems and how to prepare and present non-trial applications, whether in law school or in court.

ORGANISATION OF THE BOOK

All seven of the case studies are organised into standardised formats so that, in spite of their realism, they are easy to follow. The criminal case studies come first and the civil ones later, the logic being that bail applications and pleas in mitigation are not as complex as civil interim applications. The case studies throughout are ordered from simple to complex, so readers are advised to read them in the order presented.

Chapter 1 discusses the do's and don'ts of effective advocacy, and the key elements and techniques of oral advocacy. Chapter 2 discusses bail applications and has two case studies illustrating different approaches defence counsel might take. Chapter 3 discusses how to do a plea in mitigation against the background of two different approaches to sentencing. Each of the two case studies in this chapter focuses on one of these approaches. To prepare readers for the civil case studies, Chapter 4 is about the civil litigation process and the lawyer's function as problem solver. It discusses the stages of the civil action, the role of the interim application in it, and how to prepare and present an interim application. Chapter 5 describes a case study illustrating how to bring and defend an interim application to set aside a default judgment. Chapter 6 has a case study with a summary-judgment application. It focuses on how to use the summary judgment application as a front loading strategy and how to defend against it. Chapter 7 presents an unusual case study involving a hard fought application for interim payment. Both the applicant's aim in initiating it and the respondent's aim in defending it are to apply a high degree of pressure to the other party. Finally, Chapter 8 discusses ethics and the effect that ethical decision making has on the quality of advocacy.

THE SETTING OF THE CASE STUDIES

Information about Metroland

For simplicity's sake, all the case studies take place in the fictional country of Metroland. Metroland is a country in the Commonwealth of approximately the same area as Ireland and a population of about 20 million. Its capital is Metrocity, which is also its largest city. Its currency is the Metroland dollar, which is equal in value to the US dollar. It is a developed country with a standard of living similar to England.

Metroland has a common law system and English style criminal and civil justice systems. In the criminal justice system, the presumption of innocence is the system's touchstone. In a bail application, the onus is on the prosecution to show why bail should not be granted. A guilty plea will usually gain the defendant a lighter sentence than a not-guilty plea followed by a trial with witnesses. Most lesser offences are tried in the magistrates' court, where the magistrate is addressed as *Sir* or *Madam* or, less often, *Your Worship*. More serious crimes are tried in the county court, where the judge is addressed as *Your Honour*, and in the Supreme Court, where the judge is addressed as *My Lord* or *My Lady*.

As with many other jurisdictions, Metroland is undergoing reform in its civil justice system. It is trying to make its system more efficient and accessible and has incorporated some of the features of the Woolf reforms and the English Civil Procedure Rules 1998. Like the English Civil Procedure Rules, Metroland's Civil Procedure Rules (MCPR) must be interpreted to give effect to the overriding objective of enabling the court to deal with cases justly. In achieving this objective, as in England, the courts are empowered to save expense, ensure that the parties are on an equal footing and deal with cases in ways that are proportionate to the amount of money involved, the importance of the case, the complexity of the issues and the financial position of the parties. Where rule numbers are referred to in the civil case studies, these rules correspond to those in the 2000 edition of the English Civil Procedure Rules.

Metroland has retained a few practices that have been discarded in England, but retained in other places. Although plaintiffs are now *claimants* in Metroland, the concept and practice of pleadings has not changed and actions are still begun by writ, pleaded in *statements of claim*, and defended in a *defence*. Disclosure of documents is still referred to as discovery and the rules relating to the right to discovery remain the same. Discovery, however, refers only to document discovery; there is no right orally to examine a party for discovery as in English Canada. For English readers, however, the retention of pleadings and discovery will not make much difference because none of the case studies in this book deals directly with pleadings or discovery.

As in England, what were once interlocutory summonses, motions and applications are now all referred to as *interim applications* or, simply, *applications*. The law relating to applications in this book is basically the same as in England. For example, in the setting aside application (Chapter 5) and the summary judgment application (Chapter 6), the Woolf-inspired standards apply, so that defendants now have a somewhat higher onus to meet to prevent claimants from getting or keeping their judgments. These standards will be discussed in greater detail in those chapters.

In Metroland, some applications are heard by a Supreme Court judge. Most, however, are heard by a Supreme Court Master, who is addressed as *Master*. All applications are heard in open court and, unless there is an order to the contrary, the public are allowed to attend. When making or defending applications, lawyers have the choice of standing or sitting, although as custom has developed to adapt to the acoustics of the Metroland courtrooms, lawyers sit when the courtroom is small and stand when the courtroom is large. On applications, lawyers are not required to submit written briefs, skeleton arguments or chronologies, unless the application is expected to take longer than two hours, the parties agree, or there is a direction to that effect. Many lawyers, however, do submit written chronologies when the situation requires it. On applications, evidence is not submitted in the form of witness statements, but in the form of sworn affidavits.

In Metroland, the legal profession is unified. Anyone qualified as a lawyer is both 'called to the bar' as a barrister and 'admitted to the Supreme Court' as a solicitor. Nevertheless, some lawyers in the large cities of Metroland tend to style themselves as 'barristers' or 'solicitors', depending on whether they see themselves as courtroom or office-bound lawyers. The lawyers referred to in this book work as barristers, but inside firms of 'barristers and solicitors'. There is one firm, *Blaise Temple and Weiler, Barristers and Solicitors*, that practises both criminal and civil litigation and whose lawyers act for several of the parties described in this book.

CHAPTER 1

ADVOCACY SKILLS

This chapter describes several elements and techniques of advocacy that are particularly relevant for non-trial advocacy. It is divided into two sections. In the first, it describes briefly four key elements of effective advocacy. In the second, it describes 10 techniques of effective oral advocacy that readers should find useful in doing non-trial advocacy.

FOUR KEY ELEMENTS OF EFFECTIVE ADVOCACY

Advocacy in court is persuading the court to accept your arguments and reject those of your opponents. Because advocacy is such a complex skill, dependent on so many other skills necessary to legal practice, it is useful to keep in mind a few basic guiding principles that apply to every form of advocacy. They are referred to here as the four key elements of effective advocacy.

1 Achievable goals; flexible strategies

It is important to identify clearly why you are going to court, what you intend to achieve there and how to go about it. To use an example, if the goal is to attract a non-custodial sentence for your client, pleading not guilty and going to trial in the faint hope of getting an acquittal is usually not the best way of achieving that goal. Defendants who try their luck with a trial and are convicted are treated less leniently than those who plead guilty. Pleading guilty and preparing a strong plea in mitigation is, in many cases, a better strategy for keeping your client out of jail. Although advocacy is about winning in court, you cannot win whatever your client wants you to win. Arguments need to be based on goals that are achievable. You should be reluctant to go to court claiming a million dollars in damages when you have only enough evidence to prove a hundred thousand.

Being a form of conflict, litigation is unpredictable and can change direction at any time. Lawyers need to be flexible, changing strategy or even adopting more realistic goals. Advocacy cannot be separated from other legal skills used in litigation, so a change in strategy can mean a change not only in courtroom strategy but in the entire strategic direction of the litigation. Consider this scenario: in an application to court brought against your client, your opponents ask for several different orders. The judge suddenly comes up with a strong argument against one of the orders your opponents are seeking that neither you nor they had anticipated. You pounce on the argument and make it your own. Just as suddenly, your opponents, somewhat flustered, ask for a short adjournment to consult their client: they are considering abandoning that part of their application. So you consult your client. You remind him that there are weaknesses in your case and now might be the perfect opportunity to bring a favourable end to the litigation by negotiating from a position of strength. Your client agrees. You suggest to your opponents a one week adjournment to sit down and negotiate. They agree and, shortly thereafter, a settlement is successfully negotiated.

2 Thorough preparation

If you are not thoroughly prepared, you will lose unless you are extremely lucky, or the other side is also unprepared – a scenario you can never count on. Thorough preparation requires the lawyer, first and foremost, to outline the right strategy to achieve the goal. Then, it requires putting together the appropriate facts and law to carry out that strategy. This does not mean putting together all the facts and all the law but, rather, being selective, so that only the relevant facts and law are used. It also means anticipating counter-arguments put by the judge or your opponent. Thorough preparation involves putting in the necessary time, and maintaining a sharp mental focus prior to, and during, court.

3 Effective communication

Ensuring that your submissions are understandable is critical. Make your argument clear and easy to understand. Effective communication means not only speaking, but also listening and observing. You need to be keenly aware of signals, whether spoken or unspoken, that the judge is giving out so that you can adapt your submission accordingly. For the same reason, you also need to listen carefully to what your opponent is saying. Effective communication is not just reciting a speech. It is delivering your message clearly, and reading and interpreting the verbal and non-verbal messages you are receiving.

Part of effective communication is knowing your audience. If possible, you should learn something about your judge. It is helpful to read the judge's previous decisions in similar cases and to ask other lawyers about their experience in front of that judge: do they know of any particular inclinations? Are they aware of how the judge prefers counsel to proceed in court? Also helpful is knowing the details of the judge's practice experience, likes and dislikes and favourite causes. Knowing the judge enhances one's ability to tell an appealing story to that judge.

4   An appealing story

If the argument is built on the three elements above, you have achieved 90% of what is required. If, in addition, the argument is appealing to the judge, then you have completed the job.

To be appealing, the argument should have both logical and emotional appeal. On a logical level, facts and law should be presented in such a way that the judge is compelled to agree with you. For example, when you argue by analogy, that is, comparing your case to another (decided) case, there must be enough relevant similarities in the facts so that the judge will be persuaded. If there is a legal principle that is in your client's favour, you need to organise the facts to fit that principle. If there are conflicts in the evidence, you need to lay them side by side and show how they ought to be reconciled in your story.

On an emotional level, your argument should be constructed so that, no matter how unattractive your client may seem, it appeals to the judge's humanity. To achieve this, you cannot alter the facts, but you need to present them in ways that enhance the humanity of your client:

> Your Honour, the defendant's conviction for trafficking has brought home to her the seriousness of her act. She trafficked in drugs, it is true, but only to support her own addiction. Free from drugs for the last few weeks, she can see her way out of this life. Your Honour, I am not suggesting we are dealing with a flawless human being, or that she will be free from the temptation of drugs forever. No addict can make that claim. Nevertheless, she does have qualities and abilities as described in the pre-sentence report that suggest strong reasons why she will not return to that life ...

When you reach the end of your submission, what you ask the judge for should be the natural outcome of your presentation – just like the proper ending to a good story. No one cheers for the villain; everyone wants the hero, or underdog, to win in the end. The hero may have a tragic flaw, so the outcome – the ending to the story that you advocate – should fit the way the judge views how this tragic hero should be dealt with. You need to present your client's case to the judge in a sympathetic and appealing way. Litigation is rarely so clear cut as to involve conflicts between villains and heroes, but making your client's story human and prescribing an appropriate ending to it will help to create sympathy on the part of the judge.

TEN TECHNIQUES TO REMEMBER WHEN DOING ORAL ADVOCACY

The following techniques are based on my observations as an advocacy teacher. They are particularly applicable to non-trial advocacy.

1 Speak slowly, loudly

Many lawyers just learning to speak in public speak too fast or too softly. This is usually caused by nervousness and lack of confidence, two conditions that afflict almost everyone. People often speak too fast because they want to get the whole thing over with as quickly as possible. People often speak too softly because they lack confidence in what they are saying. Nervousness and lack of confidence can be alleviated in a number of ways:

- be thoroughly prepared and confident that you are;
- take a deep breath before speaking;
- conjure up a benign image of the judge;
- force yourself to pause after a point. This helps to slow you down and gives you time to think. It also allows the judge to absorb what you have said or to take notes;
- be comfortable with silence: refrain from breaking it unless you have a good reason;
- when you see the judge frown or strain to hear, raise your voice and slow your speech;
- if your mind goes blank, say: 'My Lord, I wonder if I might have a moment.' Take a breath and review your notes;
- force yourself to speak more slowly and to stop occasionally;
- practice with colleagues and ask for feedback.

2 Maintain eye contact

It is important to maintain eye contact so that you can gauge what the judge is thinking. For example, if the judge looks confused, this might necessitate a pause where you could say: 'Perhaps I haven't expressed that point very clearly.' If the judge, listening to a point, nods in agreement, you might say: 'I can see your Honour is with me on that point. I'll move on ...'

New lawyers sometimes fail to make eye contact because they are reading from a prepared text. Reading is not communicating. Most judges find it difficult to follow an argument that is being read aloud. Do not read from a prepared text. Jot down the major points on a single sheet of paper to remind yourself what they are. Rehearse your argument well so that you know it well. Even if you are inexperienced, you will be more persuasive speaking haltingly than reading from a text.

Many experienced counsel outline topics with highlighted headings of each topic or sub-topic. These can be supplemented with factual points and key phrases or ways of articulating key arguments that are written out in full. When counsel have dealt with a topic, they look down at their notes to ensure they have not left something out. This helps counsel to regain composure and avoid reading. It also helps them to think flexibly and modify the presentation in order to address whatever queries the judge may have.

3 Be attentive to personal appearance and behaviour

Some advocacy experts suggest that the reason advocates need to be conservatively dressed in court is so that they show respect for the dignity of the court. This is undoubtedly true. But, it is also true that, as an advocate, you should do nothing that will distract the judge from the content of your argument. You do not want the judge to be distracted by your rings or jacket when you are making your best point.

For the same reason, you should control nervous fidgeting, facial tics and other idiosyncratic gestures when you speak. Take the opportunity to view yourself on video or in the mirror when you speak so that you can identify and reduce any nervous mannerisms you may have.

At all times, be unfailingly courteous to the judge and to opponents. Make it part of your daily mode of operation. Remain restrained and dignified during your opponent's submissions, no matter how provocative your opponent's statements may be. If your opponent has misstated the evidence, you will have an opportunity to reply. Like inappropriate dress, discourtesy is distracting. If you show resentment, this will distract the judge from your argument and focus attention on you. The last thing you want is for the judge to judge you and not your case. If getting the sympathy of the court is one of your main goals, then discourtesy is obviously counter-productive.

But, what is discourteous and what isn't? There are obvious forms of discourtesy that exist in and outside the courtroom. But there are some peculiar to the courtroom. For example, using standard forms of courtroom expression is helpful in avoiding discourtesy.[1] Because different jurisdictions have different standard forms of expression, these should be learned through observation in your local courts.

4 Keep it simple

When counsel starts off with 'Your Honour, there are five issues that need to be dealt with here ...', the judge is more likely to groan inwardly than sit up and take notice. Students often wonder, what is the optimum number of issues? My answer is *'one'*, and sometimes *'two'*. It is a well known fact that, as the number of issues increases, the judge's enthusiasm for your argument decreases.

---

1   A useful book on this subject, however, is Evans, K, *The Language of Advocacy*, 1998, London: Blackstone.

If there are many issues in a case, how does one distil them? Some advocacy experts advise keeping two of the most important ones, and discarding the rest. There may be a better way. Chances are many of the issues overlap or are similar. To identify the one or two key issues, you need to be able to look at the case as a whole. Then, you should be able to summarise the main argument in one sentence. This argument should appeal to the judge logically and emotionally, yet be uniquely applicable to your client.

When you follow this process, you are actually developing the essence of the argument or *a theory of the case*. A theory of the case is the story that appeals logically and emotionally to the court.

Some examples of case theories in non-trial applications are as follows:

- 'My client should get bail because there are holes in the prosecution's case and he is the sole breadwinner.'

- 'My client should not receive a prison sentence because he is more likely to refrain from petty crime in future if he goes into an effective drug rehabilitation programme.'

- 'My client should get summary judgment because the defendant's affidavit is filled with inconsistencies and excuses.'

- 'My client should get an interim injunction, because he can never be compensated for the damage to his business that the defendant is causing.'

5 Think structurally

Once you have identified a theory of the case, you can structure your presentation to 'prove' the theory. Individual points, which appear to be unrelated, can be arranged so that they form a supporting framework for your theory. Every theory or argument requires a structure and, in this book, you will find various structural models to help you put together your argument. These models are intended to be flexible guides to preparation and not rigid protocols. They should not be slavishly followed.[2]

6 Lead the judge

When presenting a case, it is counsel's responsibility to lead the judge, not the other way around. This is an aspect of effective communication with which many new lawyers have difficulty. It shows up particularly in the way they use documents to support their argument. Documents are always part of the argument in civil non-trial applications and often in criminal ones. It is

---

2   There are three structural guides in this book: bail applications, pp 15–18; pleas in mitigation, pp 44–46; and interim applications, pp 74–79.

counsel's job to lead the judge in reviewing the various documents at critical stages of the argument. Inexperienced advocates often fail to do this. Sometimes they do not provide the judge with copies of the documents to which they are referring. Or, they assume the judge has read and remembers all the documents. Or, they assume the judge is able to find the relevant information in the relevant document as quickly as counsel.

The following are points to remember when using documents:

- Always provide the judge with a clean copy of whatever you are going to refer to – preferably in a tabbed bundle.

- When referring to a specific passage, always *lead* the judge to it: 'I wonder if I could bring your Honour to tab 3 of the bundle, the defendant's affidavit. [*Wait for the judge to find it.*] Page 4, para 9, your Honour. [*Before reading or discussing it, make sure the judge has it in sight.*] Does your Honour see the words, 'On Wednesday, 12 February …?'.

- Then bring the focus to that passage. You can do it by summarising it and letting the judge take a quick look at it. Or you can lead the judge to read it and then you can discuss it. In some situations, especially when the passage is short, it is useful to read the passage aloud for emphasis. Good counsel sometimes like to do this, especially when the passage is from an opponent's evidence and the words used are consistent with what counsel is arguing.

Leading the judge is taking the judge through the argument, step by step, and pointing out important issues that you want the judge to consider. On a few rare occasions, you may find yourself in front of judges who require little leading. They may indicate that they have read all the documents carefully, remember the facts, understand the issues and are familiar with the relevant cases. They may also indicate they want you to forgo the niceties and get on with it. In such a situation, you may decide to speed up your argument, if you are confident the judge has absorbed all your points.

But judges like these are the exception, rather than the rule. The rule is always to lead the judge.

7 Use transitional devices

A different aspect of leading the judge, but one that is important enough to require special emphasis, is the technique of using transitional devices in argument. Inexperienced lawyers tend to forget this and race from point to point before the judge realises a new point is being discussed. When moving on to a new point, remember to provide a polite transition followed by a topic label: 'I wonder, your Honour, if I could move on to my next point?' [*Transition.*] 'This concerns the issue of the defendant's colour of right.' [*Topic label.*] In this way, the judge is alerted to a new train of argument and can focus accordingly.

Another technique beginners have difficulty with is using transitions and labels when enumerating points. Some common errors may include enumerating several points and addressing them without saying which point is being addressed, or addressing points in a different sequence from the original enumeration.

What follows is a template for the way it should be done:

There are two issues that I invite your Honour to consider as the most important in this case: *first*, did the defendant have knowledge, and *second*, if so, did she deliberately mislead the claimant?

In relation to the first issue, the extent of the defendant's knowledge ... [*Counsel makes a submission on this issue.*]

I wonder if I might then go on to the second issue which relates to whether the defendant deliberately misled the claimant?

Note that each new issue is introduced with a transition and a topic label as well as a numeric label. This makes it easy for the judge to follow.

8   Focus on facts

Most new lawyers tend to focus on the law and not the facts. They tend to cite legal principles with few supporting facts because they are unfamiliar with the process of identifying important facts and applying the law to those facts. When formulating argument, it is important to focus on the facts. This way, the lawyer can construct an argument that is both human and unique, providing the emotional appeal necessary to effective persuasion (see above, p 3).[3]

9   Use law appropriately

Although the focus should be on the facts, the advocate's argument should still refer to legal principle. Using law effectively in argument depends to a great extent on effective research. Citing a case that has been overruled or is not binding in your jurisdiction is unlikely to be persuasive. Once you have got the right cases in hand, you need to argue by analogy. This means you demonstrate how the principles of the cited case apply to your case because of factual similarities. (Argument by analogy is covered above, p 3 and in case study 4, *R v Grabowski*, below, p 54.) To use law in a persuasive way you should observe the following:

---

3   Many specific techniques exist for focusing on the facts. These are referred to in relation to all the case studies. Eg, to focus on facts in a bail application, see below, pp 18–19; to focus on facts in affidavits, see below, pp 77–78.

- When citing a case, you must have a detailed knowledge of the facts of the cited case. The purpose of citing a case is to assert that the principle in that case applies to your case because the relevant facts are analogous. The judge will remain unconvinced unless you can clearly demonstrate how the facts of your case are similar to those in the cited case. Even subtle differences between the facts will influence how the judge will reach a decision. When the judge asks you about the facts of the cited case, you must be well versed enough to discuss the finer details. Your knowledge will help to support your argument.

- For the same reason, you should avoid citing secondary sources, for example, textbooks or articles, unless the principles they cite are new or very well known and widely applicable. Legal principles are abstract. To bring them to life and enhance their persuasive power, they should be illustrated with concrete, factual examples – actual cases decided by judges.

- You may need to grapple with a legal principle at a deeper level. When referring to one, you should be able to demonstrate an understanding of the purpose (or policy) behind it – whether that purpose is economic, political, social or otherwise – and how that purpose influenced the historical development of the principle. Legal principles are developed through legislation or the courts to express society's values or to create rules to reconcile conflicts between different interests. Underlying each principle is the intent to deter injustice or to do justice in the reconciliation of interests. For example, the purpose of the principle that people who cause damage to others are only responsible for it if they are negligent is to deter negligence and to encourage carefulness. The purpose of the principle that criminal defendants get out on bail unless there are good reasons to the contrary is the deep rooted presumption of innocence. These purposes are essentially moral ones, developed to produce a just, if not perfect, result in a situation of conflict. Knowing the purpose behind a legal principle enables the advocate to make an argument from a moral perspective, enhancing the argument's emotional appeal.

- In most non-trial matters, use no more than two or three cases in argument. Judges presiding over non-trial matters usually have long lists of matters to hear and are in a hurry. Despite this advice, many lawyers are reluctant to leave out cases that may seem relevant. They fear blame from the client for exposing weaknesses in their case or fear the court might accuse them of breaching their ethical duty to cite all relevant law. Lawyers concerned about this can provide the court with a number of cases, but refer only to a few in argument.

- Always ensure you provide copies of cases or statutes you do cite for the judge and your opponent. They must be clean and unmarked. Nothing makes a poorer impression than smudged, frayed documents.

- When referring to law, do so formally using its full, unabbreviated, citation: 'Your Honour, I invite you to consider at tab 2, *In Re Wakely and Bovrage,* nineteen ninety seven, volume sixty-four, Metroland Weekly Reports at page four hundred and sixteen.' This demonstrates respect for the precedents you are using to persuade the court.

10 Establish a positive relationship with the judge

Courtrooms are busy, stressful places. To present your argument in the best possible light, it is important to have a positive relationship with the judge. This can be achieved in three main ways:

(a) handling their interventions effectively;

(b) avoiding contentiousness;

(c) preparing for the worst.

Handling interventions

The quality of your relationship with judges is tested every time they intervene. They may be querying the facts, asking for clarification on the law, making rhetorical comments, or asking counsel to consider analogous circumstances or hypothetical situations. There are many types of intervention.

Answering questions from the bench promptly and competently is one of the best ways you can help judges do their job, leading them to the correct decision. Lawyers new to the courtroom tend to be intimidated by judges and their queries. Most assume their questions are hostile. While this may occasionally be the case, the judge's main aim is to get the job done, not to frighten or bully lawyers. It is important to remember that, as judges see it, their job is to clarify and test arguments so that they can make fair and well reasoned decisions. It is only natural, therefore, that in their questions, they tend to focus on the weakest parts of your argument. You should be prepared for these difficult questions. Regard them as an opportunity both to gain insight into the judge's thinking processes and to help the judge overcome reservations about your argument. Here are some points to remember in responding to their interventions:

- Listen carefully. There have been many occasions where counsel have not been listening to the query. So they guess the content wrongly and proceed to answer it wrongly. This often results in either confusing the judge or providing too much information that may have not been required. Do not be afraid to ask the judge to clarify or repeat the question. Alternatively, rephrase the question in your own words: 'Is your Lordship asking such and such?' This gives the judge an opportunity to correct you if you have misunderstood the query.

- Answer the query. Do not simply note or ignore the query or answer it inaccurately and then resume your submission. Many a junior lawyer has been berated for failing to respond accurately or at all to a query. If you do not know the answer, say so. If you think you can find the answer in your papers or from a client sitting in court, offer to do so. Alternatively, ask for a moment to locate the document or other information. If the judge accepts the offer, the judge will adjourn for a few moments. If it is not necessary, the judge will tell you to proceed.

- Do not delay answering the judge's questions just because you plan to deal with the query later in your argument. Answers such as 'Your Honour, I'll come to that later in my submission ...' will not endear you to the judge. It is much more responsive to say: 'I believe I see what is worrying your Honour. It might be useful to go straight to the case of *Walker versus Mullaly* at tab 1.'

- If the judge raises a point that requires a lengthy response that you had already planned to deal with later in your submission, you should still answer it. But try to give a brief answer that summarises the issue and then remind the court that you will be dealing with it in more detail later.

- The above points illustrate the importance of being flexible and not necessarily sticking to the plan. The advantage of being flexible and listening carefully to the judge is that, if it appears that the judge is leaning to one side or favours a particular argument which supports your application, you can take a detour in your argument and provide more evidence to support the point the judge is making.

- You can also use comments made by the judge to your advantage. If, for example, in questioning the opposing counsel the judge highlights a weakness in their case or mentions a point in your favour, make a note of it and use it in your submissions: 'I note that your Lordship is with me on that point ...' or 'Your Lordship has accurately identified the weakness in the defendant's argument.'

- When answering a question, do not resume your argument unless you are satisfied that the judge fully grasps your answer.

- Judges are not infallible. If the judge asks you to repeat a point because the judge was not listening attentively, be tactful and say something like, 'My Lord, allow me to put it in this way ...'.

- Similarly, if the judge makes a point that apparently contradicts your argument because the judge has missed a critical point, be diplomatic in your response. Don't say, 'But, my Lord, the real issue here is such and such ...'. Say instead, 'I follow what your Lordship is saying. Perhaps I can address that by putting it in a slightly different way ...'.

- If the judge raises a counter-principle that you think is irrefutable, you can introduce a different way of looking at the situation. You might say, 'I am grateful to your Lordship for reminding me of this long held legal principle. The question I invite your Lordship to consider, however, is this: on these facts, shouldn't this principle be overridden by another well established principle, that is …?'.

Avoiding contentiousness

When judges ask questions, they are seeking help from counsel to do their job properly. They need to make a decision and it is your job to help them do it. You need to see your job as that of a helper rather than an adversary. You may be at war with your opponent, but you are helping the judge.

One critical aspect of helpfulness that has not yet been addressed is the technique of putting your arguments in such a way that they become easy for the judge to reach a decision in your client's favour. In the case studies, the commonest manifestation of this technique is *avoiding contentiousness*. Avoiding contentiousness is putting your submissions in a way that they do not arouse doubt in, or resistance from, the judge. At a very basic level, it is presenting the information or the law in such a way that it does not invite the judge to jump up and say 'Now, wait a minute, counsel …'.

Preparing for the worst

Although avoiding contentiousness is important, on occasion, the judge's behaviour may be out of line and the atmosphere may become unavoidably contentious. For example, the judge may ask you hostile questions. The reasons the judge does this may relate to your handling of the case or to the judge's private emotions that have nothing to do with your case. Despite the judge's hostility, you must control the urge to express your resentment. Respond courteously to the question and do not show negative emotions. On rare occasions, a judge's behaviour may go beyond mere hostility into outright rudeness. The judge may be falling asleep, interrupting too often or ridiculing you or your client. While it is extremely important in the interests of your client not to get dragged into a confrontation, sometimes, counsel may have to summon the courage to speak up. In such a situation, counsel should speak firmly, but respectfully, for example:

Excuse me, my Lord, with the greatest of respect, it would be difficult for any counsel trying to do the best for his client not to take umbrage at those comments.

Though these situations are rare, one should be prepared for them.

CHAPTER 2

BAIL APPLICATION

The case studies begin with a bail application because it is one of the commonest and simplest forms of non-trial advocacy. Even when it goes beyond a 'one word' submission, the bail application is usually very brief, based on just a few principles, and is unencumbered by lengthy affidavits or other bulky documents.

To clients charged with a crime, the bail application is a crucial event, because even temporary liberty is better than jail. Liberty reinforces the hope of acquittal and facilitates the defendant's preparation of his defence. It may also enable him to raise sufficient funds to pay for a good lawyer.

Some clients, however, may prefer not to apply for bail if they know their chances of getting it are low and the likelihood of a custodial sentence high. They also know that the time served during remand will count toward their probable sentence.

THEORY OF THE CASE

As with all advocacy preparation, it is important to begin with a theory of the case – a story that is persuasive to the judge's mind and heart. For a story to be persuasive, it has to be supported by sound facts and principles. Every bail application is based on the same fundamental principle: *until proven guilty beyond a reasonable doubt, the defendant is presumed innocent.* Without the presumption of innocence, there would be little need for bail. People could be charged and put in custody immediately. By relying on the principle of presumed innocence, the lawyer doing a bail application can formulate a defence theory of *until proven guilty at trial, the client is entitled to liberty.* From this theory, the lawyer can argue for the kinds of conditions the court should impose on the client. How much liberty and under what conditions will depend on the facts of the case.

CONDITIONS

If a key part of counsel's theory is that the client is entitled to liberty until proven guilty, the prosecution's usual counter-theory is that the facts suggest he should not be given liberty or that certain conditions should be imposed on him limiting that liberty. Thus, defence counsel will argue for more liberty and fewer or less severe conditions and the prosecution will argue for less liberty and more severe conditions. There are many different kinds of conditions, some of which are not used in all jurisdictions. The most severe condition is simply no bail or a detention order. The least severe is the defendant merely signs a promise or undertaking to appear. In between those two extremes are a variety of conditions. The following are several of the most common conditions.

Cash bail

This is the deposit of a sum of money by the defendant or his surety (see below) as a condition of bail.

Sureties

The surety guarantees the appearance of the defendant at court on the specified day. The surety may do so by paying the cash bail or by entering into a recognisance guaranteeing payment in the event that the defendant does not appear.

Other conditions

Other common conditions include reporting at a police station at specified intervals; residing at a particular location; prohibition on leaving the jurisdiction and/or surrender of passport; prohibition on visiting certain areas or approaching certain witnesses.

PRINCIPLES AND ARGUMENTS

The prosecution will rely on one or more principles to persuade the court not to grant bail or to grant it but with conditions attached. A variety of these principles exist, but included here are three of the most commonly used.

Principles

(1) The defendant is unlikely to appear for trial.
(2) The defendant is likely to commit an offence while on bail.
(3) The defendant is likely to interfere with witnesses.

The prosecution and defence will submit a variety of arguments to support or oppose the application of these principles. These will depend on the facts of the case and the defendant's individual circumstances. A few common examples are as follows.

Arguments

- *The defendant's roots in the community*: if the defendant has roots in the community, he is less likely to abscond. Thus, a married man with a family who has steady employment is arguably more likely to appear for trial than an unemployed single man with no job and no family in the vicinity (principle 1 above).
- *The strength of the case against the defendant*: the stronger the case, the more likely the defendant will be convicted. If a conviction is more likely, then the defendant arguably will be more motivated not to appear for trial (principle 1 above).
- *The seriousness of the offence*: the more serious the offence, the more likely it will warrant a lengthy custodial sentence. With this possibility in mind, it can be argued that the defendant will be motivated to abscond (principle 1 above).
- *The defendant's criminal record*: the defendant's previous convictions (or antecedents) will affect his sentence if he is convicted. Certain factors will be taken into account: the number of convictions for similar offences, the number of convictions for all offences, the nature of previous sentences and his most recent conviction. The more damaging his criminal record is, the more likely it is that his custodial sentence will be longer and, arguably, the more likely it is he will consider absconding (principle 1 above). If he has a previous history of absconding, this will obviously weaken his argument that he is likely to appear for trial. If he has a previous conviction for an offence that occurred while he was on bail on a previous occasion, this will weaken his argument that he is unlikely to commit an offence while on bail on this occasion (principle 2 above). Obviously, if the defendant has a clear record, his lawyer should stress this fact.
- *The defendant knows prosecution witnesses*: the defendant knows how to contact prosecution witnesses and there is evidence to suggest likely intimidation (principle 3 above).

STRUCTURE

Like a good story, a good argument needs a structure. Structure is important to draw the listener into the argument, to make it more logical and understandable. New lawyers sometimes mistakenly assume that judges impose rules of structure and that they need to be followed rigidly. This, of course, is not the case. Rules of structure should allow flexibility and be modified to suit the goals of the argument. The only test of whether a structure is appropriate is whether or not it is persuasive. Outlined below is a step by step structure which defence counsel can use or modify for a bail application.

Structure of a bail application

1   State nature of application, offences charged
2   Explain accused's position on charge
3   Identify legal principles on which application is based
4   Use relevant facts to support argument on each principle
5   Describe defendant's relevant personal circumstances
6   Summarise concisely and request appropriate order

The following is an example of how this structure can be used in a bail application.

Example

The charge is wounding with intent. The victim, a young man now in hospital, was stabbed twice – once in the shoulder and once in the abdomen – in what appears to be a gang fight. The accused was arrested in the vicinity, 10 feet from a knife that was used in the stabbing. He admitted he knew some people involved in the fight, but denied he was a member of any gang, that he was involved in the stabbing, and that the knife was his. He said he was walking in that area to go to a shop when he stopped to watch the fight. The prosecution alleged he had a previous conviction for assault six years ago and one for shoplifting two years ago.

1   State nature of application, offences charged

    Counsel: I appear before you on behalf of the defendant to make an application for bail. The accused has been charged with one count of wounding with intent.

2   Explain accused's position on charge

    Counsel: I am instructed that the defendant will be pleading not guilty to the charge. He intends to defend the charge and proceed to trial.

3 Identify legal principles on which application is based

Counsel: Sir, I understand the prosecution intends to oppose t.
application; they are of the view that, because of the seriousness
of the offence, they question the likelihood of my client
appearing for trial.

4 Use relevant facts to support argument on each principle

Counsel: Sir, the offence is indeed a serious one. Nevertheless, the
evidence that the prosecution are relying on is purely
circumstantial, suggesting my client has a strong defence. There
is no reason for him to abscond.

If I may briefly highlight some of the obvious weaknesses in the
prosecution's evidence, then proceed to deal with my client's
personal circumstances and bail conditions.

Sir, dealing first with the weaknesses in the evidence. May I
refer you to page one of the police report, about half way down
the first page. You will see that, although the accused was
found by the police in the vicinity of the fight, no eyewitnesses
identifying the accused have been produced. I am sure the
prosecution will also confirm that there is no fingerprint
evidence implicating my client. He has emphatically denied his
involvement, informing the police at the scene and under
caution at the police station that he was on his way to the shop
that night when he came upon this fight. This statement is
consistent with his behaviour: while others fled from the scene,
my client stayed put. Furthermore, he has co-operated with the
police and made himself available on four occasions for identity
parades. On the evidence gathered so far, I submit that a
conviction is hardly assured.

5 Describe defendant's relevant personal circumstances

Counsel: Now, on to his personal circumstances which also support the
likelihood of my client appearing for trial. Madam prosecutor
has provided you, Sir, with my client's criminal record. May I
stress that the first conviction was over six years ago and
should be treated as spent, while the second is not similar to the
present offence. I respectfully invite the court to give it little
weight or, indeed, disregard it completely for the purposes of
this application. Additionally, I am instructed to inform the
court that, on both previous occasions, my client appeared at all
hearings and there has been no history of absconding.

In relation to possible bail conditions, may I assist the court by
saying that, although my client has very little savings and is

unable at this stage to secure someone in a position to act as surety, he does have strong roots in the local community. He was born in this city and has lived here all his life. He is single and lives with his brother not far from here at 1907 Calder Avenue. In relation to his employment, Sir, until recently he worked as a delivery worker at Five Continents Moving and Storage. Unfortunately, he has been made redundant along with a number of co-workers as a result of the downturn in the moving business. He is actively seeking employment in this city, however, and he tells me that he has two job interviews scheduled for this afternoon.

Magistrate: Counsel, what type of jobs is he applying for and what approximate salary is he expecting?

Counsel: Sir, may I have a moment to clarify my instructions on that point.

[*Counsel confers with client.*]

Counsel: Sir, the defendant has interviews at a construction site and at a local supermarket. Unfortunately, he is unclear about the salary expected. However, I suspect it would be close to the minimum wage. In the event he secures employment the defendant is prepared to use part of his salary towards any cash bail should the court seek to impose such a condition.

Sir, the defendant is a motivated, responsible individual who provides a financial contribution to his brother when he is able. He has a steady employment history and, from my conversations with him, it appears all his friends and contacts live here.

6 Summarise concisely and request appropriate order

Counsel: In conclusion, Sir, there is not only a likelihood he will appear for his trial, but a strong likelihood he will do so. My client is prepared to comply with reasonable bail conditions the court sees fit to impose; however, may I submit that appropriate conditions under the circumstances should be that he be released on his own recognisance and report at the Central Metrocity police station once a week between 5 and 9 pm. Finally, my client is prepared to surrender his travel document. Unless I can clarify any further points, Sir, that is my application.

FOCUSING ON THE FACTS

One of the challenges for new lawyers is to identify relevant facts of the case and link them to the basic principles. For example, the most basic principle of the above case is that the defendant is presumed innocent until proven guilty. Therefore, he should get bail unless the prosecution can show he is likely to abscond. It is the defence counsel's job to put forward facts that suggest the defendant is *not* likely to abscond.

In the above case, defence counsel argued that the evidence as set out in the police report was weak. He wanted to demonstrate that a weak case would motivate the accused not to abscond, but to go to court to defend himself. Counsel did not – and, at this point, should not – stand up to argue that the allegations presented by the prosecution are untrue and that the client is innocent of the charge.

A bail application is not a trial. The prosecution's allegations are presented on sheets of paper, usually a police report prepared by the investigating officers. There is no opportunity or time, at this point, to call these officers as witnesses or to call other witnesses. They cannot be cross-examined, so the court cannot oversee a searching inquiry of what really happened on the day in question. At this stage, the police version and the client's version of events are bound to be dissimilar. Defence counsel should assume that what the police say is basically correct and not try to contradict it with the defendant's version. If there are no weaknesses in the prosecution case as revealed in the police version of the facts, it is best not to argue that weaknesses exist just because the client says he did not commit the crime.

On the other hand, sometimes weaknesses do exist, and this is when counsel needs to point them out – not to prove innocence, but to demonstrate that the client will be motivated to show up for trial because he is innocent and an acquittal is imminent. To make this argument, counsel has to study the facts carefully. Counsel should look first at what the police say in isolation from what the defendant says. In examining the facts, counsel should ask several questions. Are there crucial gaps in the evidence? Is the evidence circumstantial? Are there internal contradictions in the evidence? Are there any eyewitnesses? Are there vague statements by the witnesses? Is there room to expose other kinds of weaknesses in the witness statements? For example, was the lighting poor? Was it late at night? What was the distance between the witness and the criminal act? Unless defence lawyers are concerned about tipping off the prosecution to the game plan for trial, they should draw the court's attention to weaknesses in the evidence to demonstrate that the client's chances of success at trial are good.

PUTTING FACTS AND ARGUMENTS
'TO AVOID CONTENTIOUSNESS'

In order to get the judge to see things from the defence point of view, it is important for counsel to avoid contentiousness. Counsel can avoid contentiousness by pointing out weaknesses in the prosecution's facts only, and avoiding discussion of contradictory assertions by the client. In other words, counsel avoids raising issues that the judge would be inclined to disagree with. In the above submission, counsel avoids contentiousness by discussing the facts only as presented by the prosecution. He did not offer his client's version of the events, except through the police report of statements made by the defendant. If defence counsel had questioned the police version with a statement such as 'but my client told me he was not in the vicinity of where the victim was injured', this would invite contentiousness. It would make the judge pause and question what counsel is saying, because the police report says precisely the opposite. When scrutinising the accuracy of a police report, you should look at evidentiary gaps, internal contradictions, or aspects that are consistent with what your client says.

Some examples of what to say:

- 'Sir, there is some evidence in this report, but I don't see an eyewitness account. It is all circumstantial.'
- 'I notice, in the police report, one witness says the incident occurred inside the front door of 423 Prentice Road, but another said it was outside 428 Prentice Road. I bring this discrepancy to your attention, Sir, because it shows the prosecution could well have a problem with their case.'
- 'I draw your attention to the fact that the police report does say the defendant denied the theft when first questioned and continued to deny it. That, of course, is consistent with what he is saying here today: he continues to maintain his innocence and will be pleading not guilty to the charge.'

The important point about avoiding contentiousness is to ensure the process of leading the judge is not interrupted. This process should be a smooth one, during which time the judge should have little cause to sit up and disagree with you.

In the following case study, defence counsel develops a strategy for a bail application that is firmly rooted in avoiding contentiousness. The charge is resisting arrest, a charge that the police and the judge view as serious. The client is angry about the charge because he feels harassed by the police officer who tried to arrest him. The client knows the officer from previous encounters and has reason to be afraid of him.

Before going ahead with the first case study, read the section below on using the case studies.

Using the case studies

1   There are seven case studies in this book. Each outlines the facts of the case and, for the civil case studies, includes supporting documents. Following each case study are the 'solutions', which comprise the *Lawyers' strategies* and the *Oral submissions* in court. Finally, there are the *Outcome* (the court's decision) and the *Commentary*, which analyses the lawyer's approach to the case.

2   Read each case study and work on solving the problem on your own or with a colleague. To formulate your solution, use the following checklist for each 'client':

   • identify the client's goal;

   • outline the strategy you would adopt in argument;

   • identify important legal issues and the facts you would use to support them;

   • identify any advocacy techniques you would use;

   • explain how you plan to structure your arguments.

3   After formulating your own solution, read the solutions provided – the lawyers' strategies and oral submissions:

   • compare them to your own; note similarities and differences;

   • evaluate whether the oral submissions are effective.

4   Outline what the outcome should be and why:

   • compare this to the actual outcome;

   • read the commentary and decide whether you agree with it.

A final note about the case studies: they employ a system of date coding. This current year is referred to as Yr0, last year as Yr–1, two years ago as Yr–2 and so on. Next year is Yr+1.

CASE STUDY 1: *R v FENNELLY*

Facts known to the prosecution and defence

Client's name: William Preston Fennelly

Address: #478–12 East Hampton Street, Metrocity

Age and marital status: 26 years old, separated

Income: $2,000 per month as a construction labourer. He is presently working as a labourer on a construction site outside Metrocity. He has $7,500 in savings.

Charge: Resisting arrest, s 42 of the Police Force Act. [Under this section: 'Any person who assaults or resists any police officer acting in the execution of his duty, or aids or incites any person so to assault or resist, or refuses to assist any such officer in the execution of his duty when called upon to do so ... shall be liable on summary conviction to a fine of $5,000 and to imprisonment for 6 months.']

Prosecution will inform the court that there is a possibility of a second charge being laid, that of possession of dangerous drugs pending the outcome of the Government's Final Chemist Laboratory report on the cigarette discarded by the defendant. The initial report lists ginseng herb as the main ingredient of the cigarette; however, nominal traces of another ingredient have been detected and tests are currently being conducted to identify it. It is suspected to be heroin hydrochloride.

Previous convictions: Yr–6 Possession of dangerous drugs (cannabis) – probation six months; Yr–5 Possession of dangerous drugs (cocaine) – two months' imprisonment; Yr–3 Theft (shop theft) – $1,000 fine and probation, one year.

Prosecution's allegations: The prosecution's allegations come from a report prepared by a police constable which contains the following:

On the evening of 26 April, Yr0, at 8:05 pm, I was patrolling in Chinatown along Fairmont Avenue. Adjacent to Fairmont Avenue is a lane well known as a hang-out for drug takers. I noticed one Caucasian male and one Asian male in the lane sitting on wooden crates sharing a cigarette. From across the street, I saw the Caucasian, whom I recognised as the defendant, Fennelly, draw on the cigarette and pass it to his Asian companion, Tang. (Tang was separately charged.) I could smell the smoke and noticed that it was strong and pungent, unlike cigarette smoke. As I approached them, I noticed the pupils of Fennelly's eyes appeared dilated.

I suspected that what they were smoking was dangerous drugs and I decided to arrest them. I walked up to them and said, 'You are under arrest'. Tang replied, 'Why? We've done nothing wrong'. I then told them that I suspected that the cigarette contained dangerous drugs. Fennelly held up the half-smoked cigarette and said, 'This is just a Chinese herbal cigarette Tang bought in a shop'.

'Come on,' I said, taking Fennelly by the arm. I then reached for Tang in an attempt to escort both of them to the police station. Tang pushed me away with great force and I fell onto one of the wooden crates. Both men ran away.

I retrieved the still smouldering cigarette from the ground and sent it to the police laboratory for testing. The initial test showed that the main substance in the cigarette was Chinese ginseng root. However, there were nominal traces of another ingredient which has not yet been identified.

This is Fennelly's second appearance in court. He was arrested last night at his mother's home. Six days have elapsed since his encounter with the police constable in the lane.

Facts known to the defence lawyers (instructions from the defendant)

Personal circumstances: Client is single, having lived with his widowed mother and one brother, a student (15 years old) for the last five years. Client has a limited education, having left school at the age of 16. Since then, he has worked at a variety of jobs, but has never had a steady job.

He is currently working at a construction site and earns about $2,000 per month. He makes a monthly contribution of $700 to his mother. His mother has a small pension, but depends to a large extent on her son's contributions. She is not able to act as surety. She is in poor health and has few financial resources.

Client owns no property, but would be prepared to put some or all of his savings toward bail. He has savings of $7,500.

The client's employer, Wynford Construction Co Ltd, has told the client's mother that, unless Fennelly returns to work in one week's time, he will be replaced. Police bail had been denied.

Client does not deny the police statement above, but strongly denies the charge. He has not yet been advised of his rights or possible defences. He says this particular police constable knows him, often harasses him on the street, and on one occasion a year ago threatened him with a beating if he continued to frequent the Chinatown area. The client said he was afraid of the policeman and of what might happen to him if he was arrested.

Client says he is reliable. He has been granted bail on three previous occasions and has never had his bail revoked or estreated for failing to appear for a court hearing.

Defence position

Client is unwilling to volunteer any bail conditions other than offering a cash deposit. He does not want to be bound by any reporting conditions because this would effect his employability. He often works 12–15 hour shifts, including overtime work, which provides him with extra money. Reporting conditions would disrupt his work and might lead to termination or at least reduction of overtime work.

Prosecution position

The prosecution will oppose bail or try to obtain stringent bail conditions. They believe Fennelly is a troublemaker and has links with a large drug trafficking syndicate. During a conversation, the prosecution told defence counsel that the police thought Fennelly and Tang smoked the cigarette within smelling distance of the constable deliberately in order to provoke him. In view of the flagrant disregard for the law, the prosecution see it as a serious offence.

Lawyer's strategy

- On the charge of resisting arrest, there may be an issue as to whether or not there was a lawful arrest. I will advise the client that he has a good chance of success at trial.

- It is obvious that the client is well known to the police and they consider him a nuisance and a troublemaker. They did not grant him police bail. The prosecution is also opposing bail. Obviously, police attitudes have influenced the prosecution's position on bail. Nevertheless, I should avoid arguing police harassment or suggesting unreasonable conduct on the part of the police. The magistrate is a former prosecutor, so such an approach is bound to be contentious. At any rate, judges usually support the police who have a dangerous job. Judges regard any kind of resistance to, or assault on, a police officer – especially a lone officer on duty – as a serious matter.

- Instead of alleging harassment, what I can do is lead the judge by conceding that the charge is serious. Then, I will equalise the concession by using an expression that is tried and true in the magistrates' court and certainly appropriate in this situation: *although resisting arrest is a serious offence, what the defendant did was not a serious example of this offence* and is therefore unlikely to attract a custodial sentence. Of course, I will remind the court that he has a good defence to the charge in any event. The defence is that the police officer did not have reasonable grounds for believing my client was committing an offence.

- In fact, I want to imply the offence is trivial, without forcing the magistrate to adopt that view publicly. In making my argument, I have to be diplomatic so as not to devalue the role of the police in the proper execution of their duties. I have to pay special attention to this in my presentation of facts.

Oral submission

[*The prosecution read out the charge, and supporting facts. It stated that it regards this as a serious offence in view of the daily exposure to physical risk that police officers face. It is opposing bail. To the unpleasant surprise of defence counsel, Mr Blaise, the prosecution adopted an alternative position, saying that it requires a two week adjournment to await the analysis of the police laboratory report on traces of the unidentified substance in the cigarette. Only then could it determine whether a second charge should be added, that of possession of a dangerous drug. Defence counsel rises to deliver his submission.*]

Defence counsel: Sir, I appear before you to make an application for bail on behalf of the defendant. Allow me to begin by reassuring you that there is no suggestion by the defence that resisting arrest is a less-than-serious offence. I hope you will agree with me that, in this instance, the allegations resulting in the charge fall on the lower end of the scale of seriousness.

But, on an application for bail, the important question we have to ask is, how serious is the offence? The more serious it is, the more likely it is that the defendant may abscond. The less serious it is, the less serious will be the punishment. And the more likely it is the defendant will appear for trial.

What my client is alleged to have done in this case is by no means trivial, but it is also not a serious example of this type of offence for two reasons: first, my client's alleged resistance was merely that he ran away. He did not use any force.

Second: he was running away from being arrested for a suspected crime that the prosecution have produced no evidence to support.

In relation to the first reason, according to the prosecution, it wasn't my client who pushed the officer, it was Mr Tang. In fact, my client appears to have been very co-operative at first. He let the police officer arrest him without objection. When Tang pushed the officer and ran, however, my client panicked and ran as well. He is a fearful person and, given his previous convictions, his fear of being arrested after the police officer was pushed was understandable. He was afraid of being arrested. This is not to suggest fear of being arrested is an excuse – it just explains his actions.

This leads me to the second reason for suggesting this is not a serious example of this type of offence. The cigarette he and his companion are said to have been smoking contained ginseng root and this was consistent with what he told the police officer. He was not doing anything unlawful at the time. Again, this is not an excuse, but it is something to consider.

Even if he is convicted on the charge of resisting arrest, I doubt whether this conviction would result in a custodial sentence. Furthermore, my client is going to plead not guilty, and, although I have not yet had time to study the case carefully, on the facts the prosecution has presented so far, he does appear to have a good defence.

[*Counsel pauses.*]

There is one more matter, Sir: the prosecution, it seems, have a fallback position. If they do not succeed in getting a detention order, they are requesting a two week adjournment in the hope that further analysis of nominal amounts of a yet-to-be-identified ingredient will provide them with evidence to lay a second charge against my client. In the meantime, they want to keep him in custody.

Sir, while I can appreciate the prosecution's concern, keeping him in custody for another night, let alone two weeks, is simply not appropriate in a case such as this. For one thing, they've already done a laboratory test on this ingredient and the results are inconclusive. For another, the cigarette has already been in the laboratory for a week. Finally, Sir, even if the police lab does come up with a dangerous-drug finding, and there is sufficient evidence to lay a second charge, the amount detected would certainly not warrant a custodial sentence.

At this stage, I should say a little bit about my client's background, so that I can suggest appropriate bail conditions. He has strong roots in the community. He lives with his widowed mother on East Hampton Street in Metrocity. They have been at that address for five years. He gives a monthly contribution of $700 to his mother. She is unable to act as surety because she has no financial resources. I am instructed that he has savings of $7,500, so he can put up cash bail, if necessary.

Sir, this is a man who has not been in trouble with the police for three years. He's holding a steady job and it would clearly be in the community's interest for him to keep that job. He is a construction worker now working on a construction site, with a salary of about $2,000 a month. The client's employer, Wynford Construction Co Ltd, has informed him that if he does not return to work in a week's time he will be terminated. In addition, since he works regular overtime, he requests the court's indulgence not to impose reporting conditions as this will disrupt his shifts and could result in him being dismissed. Instead of reporting to the police, he is prepared to provide cash bail, if necessary. May I suggest $500? Unless I can be of further assistance, those are my submissions.

Outcome

The magistrate agreed with no reporting conditions, but set cash bail at $1,000.

Commentary

In making an argument so as to avoid contentiousness, one technique used by counsel, Mr Blaise, is to make a concession: '… there is no suggestion by the defence that resisting arrest is a less than serious offence.' But as with most concessions made during the course of effective advocacy, this one is short lived. Counsel equalises it immediately when he says resisting arrest may be a serious offence, but this incident is not a 'serious example' of this type of offence.

Concessions are a key ingredient of effective advocacy because they help to reflect what is actually taking place in the court's mind. The court has to make a decision and it needs to weigh different arguments to make that decision. The court is saying to itself 'on one hand ... but on the other hand ...' while trying to identify an overriding principle or fact. This is not an easy job, yet counsel can make it easier by reflecting the process of weighing and reasoning that leads to the correct conclusion. When counsel makes a concession, he is showing that he has looked at both sides of the argument. He is showing the court how to weigh them in its own mind. Counsel is thus helping the judge to do the difficult job of making a decision.

This 'helpfulness' aspect of effective advocacy, of which concessions and avoiding contentiousness are prime examples, needs to be ingrained in lawyers. To some lawyers, the judge in a courtroom is a remote and threatening authority figure who does not require help. This way of perceiving the judge creates fear and antagonism. Lawyers have to recognise that judges have a job to do and the advocate's approach must be based on helping them to do that job – but in ways that will persuade them to see things from the advocate's viewpoint. Being helpful to the judge is far more persuasive than being antagonistic.

Keith Evans, in his book, *The Golden Rules of Advocacy*, explains the helpfulness principle through something he dubs the Sympathy Rule. The Sympathy Rule begins with trying to put yourself in the judge's shoes. You need to try to see and hear what the judge sees and hears and develop sympathy for judges in their difficult role. When advocates show they have sympathy for the judge, it will be reciprocated. Once counsel gets this kind of rapport underway, the judge is much more likely to listen carefully, put a kinder interpretation on what counsel says and even feel inclined to overlook counsel's mistakes.

When you follow the Sympathy Rule, Evans explains, you avoid confrontations – confrontations that arise when counsel pushes too hard, or makes demands. These approaches provoke resistance. One way of minimising resistance is to choose the language of advocacy carefully. Counsel should *invite* and not demand. Counsel should *suggest* and not tell.[1] Counsel should *request* and not direct. Counsel should be *grateful* to her Ladyship for raising the issue rather than telling her the question she just asked is not relevant. Counsel should *submit* or *respectfully submit* and not opine or think. In court, counsel should refer to opponents as *my learned friend*, not necessarily because they are either learned or friendly, but because it communicates to the court that you respect your opponent. If your opponent is learned and worthy of a hearing, then so are you. The battle raging underneath all the fine language may be fierce, but to lose control and let your emotions run amuck is to lose persuasive power. Adopting the accepted formal rhetoric of the courtroom does not mean you have become subservient or obsequious or even that you are just 'playing the game'. It means, simply, that you respect the system as well as the people involved in making difficult decisions. That respect will be reciprocated.

---

1   Evans, K, *The Golden Rules of Advocacy*, 1993, London: Blackstone, pp 55–56.

In the *Fennelly* case, defence counsel could easily have become angry when the prosecution surprised counsel by asking for a two week adjournment. Less experienced counsel might have become emotional or discourteous, telling the court they had been caught by surprise and suggesting that the police were persecuting their client. For the prosecution to ask for a two week adjournment in this situation was undoubtedly provocative, but this counsel stayed in control. He continued respectfully to list the arguments against it, stressing the less-than-serious nature of the offence without saying it was trivial.

Only by staying in control can counsel be in a position to help the judge. Inexperienced counsel are prone to become agitated and perhaps speak too fast in order to get the whole unpleasant experience over with as soon as possible. Sometimes, they argue with judges when they intervene, or try to convince them of the rightness of their argument, even when judges make it plain that they see no merit in it. Or, they present too much information, overwhelming the judge with detail and arguments.

In the following bail application, the advocate has a more difficult job to do because the offence is much more serious. In this case, the defendant is caught at the airport with a large quantity of heroin and, unlike the first two cases, the facts seem completely against him. There does not appear to be a defence. But, the lawyer develops a theory of the case and a way of presenting that theory that helps the judge to reach a decision.

CASE STUDY 2: *R v BALSAM*

Facts known to the prosecution and defence

Client's name: Jeremy Balsam

Address: #32–423 High Wind Road, Metrocity

Age and marital status: 20 years old, single

Income: None. He is a third year science student at the University of Metroland. He has $5,000 in savings from his part time jobs.

Charge: Trafficking in dangerous drugs (heroin), s 5 of the Dangerous Drugs Act. [Under this section: '... no person shall, on his own behalf or on behalf of another, traffic in dangerous drugs ...' Under the interpretation section of this Act, trafficking includes selling, importing, exporting or possessing for the purpose of trafficking. Cases under this statute have decided that knowledge is presumed when dangerous drugs are found in the custody or control of the accused and that trafficking is presumed when the dangerous drug is found in a large quantity. The section provides for a maximum sentence of life imprisonment.]

Previous convictions: None.

Prosecution's allegations: On Saturday 3 November, Yr0, the defendant was observed to be behaving in a nervous manner while waiting to check in his luggage at the Metro Airways counter at the airport. Customs officials, on duty in the departures concourse, watched him for about 15 minutes. He left the queue twice to go to the washroom, leaving his luggage unattended both times. After he checked his luggage in, one officer retrieved it, while another questioned the defendant. During this conversation, the defendant identified the luggage as his. He agreed to a body and luggage search. During the luggage search, which was conducted with the assistance of a police dog, the officers discovered the luggage had a false bottom with a small compartment. In the compartment was a wooden smoked salmon gift box. The box contained 10 zippered plastic bags filled with a white powdered substance. The bags weighed a total of two and one-third kilograms. The white substance was later analysed at the Metrocity police laboratory and was identified as heroin hydrochloride.

When the false bottom was discovered, the defendant said: 'This is very strange. Why did he do this? This luggage belongs to someone else.' The defendant was immediately placed under arrest and cautioned. He said nothing further in relation to the charge, but did reveal information about his family and personal circumstances.

After enduring a night in jail and a police interview, the defendant was able to telephone his father, who came down to the police station with his lawyer. Bail was negotiated with the police, who fixed it at $5,000 cash deposit, including surrender of the defendant's passport. The police issued the defendant a summons to appear in court in four days' time.

Personal circumstances: The defendant is a Metroland citizen with a valid Metroland passport. He lives in a small rooming house with other students near Metrocity University. His mother and father are divorced. The father lives in Metrocity and is a prosperous optician. He is giving his son considerable financial help to attend university. The defendant is the youngest of three children; the other two live with their mother in New York. The police are not aware that the defendant has any criminal connections.

Facts known to the defence lawyers (instructions from the defendant)

The client says that he was not behaving nervously in the check-in queue, but had to go to the washroom several times because he was suffering from diarrhoea.

The client says he was on his way to his sister's wedding in New York. He has one week of term break holidays. He said he had borrowed the luggage from another student and did not know about the drugs or the false bottom. His own luggage had been stolen. He is unwilling to disclose the name of this student at this stage, although he may do so later. The client does not object to providing the court with any of this information. The client said, without being asked, that he has a previous conviction for marijuana possession. He pleaded guilty in a New Jersey courtroom last year and received a fine of US $300. He said that, during the summer, when he was visiting his mother in New York, he went to a party in New Jersey and was arrested in a police raid. He was not deported.

Defence position

The client does not want to go to jail because he wants to complete his studies. His father will act as surety and is prepared to offer as much as $50,000 in cash or undertakings (but would be prepared, if necessary, to put up his house as security, the value of which is $300,000). The client is prepared to surrender his passport and would, if required, report to the police daily.

Prosecution position

The defendant has been on police bail, but preliminary investigations by the police suggest that they have a 'strong case' against the client. Prosecution will, therefore, oppose an application for continued bail. The amount of heroin involved is large. Prosecution consider the charges of attempting to export and trafficking to be very serious.

Lawyer's strategy

- The prosecution does appear to have a strong case. The substantive issue on the charge is, did the defendant know the heroin was in this luggage? On the face of it, knowledge can easily be attributed to my client. So, when I make the bail application, I have to avoid facts that remind the judge of just how strong the case is. At this stage, there is little to suggest that there is a good defence to the charge. The stronger the case is against my client, and the more serious the charge, the more reason he has to abscond. That is why 'strength of case' and 'seriousness of the offence' are relevant factors when considering a bail application. My client appears to have every motivation to abscond, and with a mother in New York, he can easily disappear.

- Two important features of this case, however, suggest an argument that nicely counters 'seriousness' and 'strength of case', yet avoids confronting head on the incident at the airport. The first is that the police gave him police bail, so, for the last few days, he has been free on bail, evidently trusted by the police that he will obey the summons and show up for court. Do the police know something that I don't know? Did they take a less serious view of the defendant's involvement in the crime when he was arrested, and now are assuming a tougher stance to put pressure on him? Was he set up? Were the drugs placed in his luggage without his knowledge? These are the sort of doubts I want to plant in the judge's mind without describing them explicitly. I do not want to make any speculative or contentious allegations that would inevitably invite counter-argument, or even rebuke, from the bench. On the other hand, I do want to remind the judge that the defendant has already complied with relatively mild bail conditions and shown up for court.

- The second important feature of the case is that this is an unusual defendant – a university student in his third year, with no prior convictions in Metroland and no criminal connections. It is rare for such a promising person to get involved in serious crime. I want to remind the judge of this and then put the two features together, suggesting that the police may have granted bail to the defendant precisely because they, too, were struck by how unusual this defendant was and how unlikely it would be for him to abscond. I want to try to turn the tables on the prosecution taking the spotlight off the airport incident and shining it on the actions of the police.

- I will not be saying anything about the New Jersey conviction for marijuana possession.

Oral submission

[*The prosecution has read out the charge, supporting facts and its position on bail. Defence counsel, Ms Calhoun, then rises to make her application.*]

Defence counsel: Sir, this is an application for bail. As you know, Mr Balsam has been charged with one count of trafficking under s 5 of the Dangerous Drugs Act.

The prosecution oppose bail because they say the charge is serious. I would like to point out that my client is a promising young man. The prosecution have not alleged any convictions and you can see from the papers that the police, in their investigations, have not found him to be involved with any known criminals or in any criminal activity. It is evident that he will present no danger to society if granted bail. What the prosecution do seem to be suggesting, however, is that he is unlikely to show up for his trial and that, therefore, he ought to be detained in custody. This is the issue that needs to be dealt with.

There is no denying that the charge is serious. But, two important points need to be made. The first point is that, I think everyone would agree, this is an unusual defendant to be charged with an offence of this nature. A 20 year old student, who has made it successfully through to his third year at our most prestigious university, from a reputable family entangled in something that young men such as this do not usually get involved in. That is not to say that just because people are university students they do not get into trouble. They can, and the courts have, I'm sure, encountered such cases. There are, nevertheless, some very unusual features surrounding the facts of this case and there may be more to it than meets the eye.

I submit, Sir, that the police may have viewed it in much the same way. They, too, may have seen this defendant as a very untypical defendant. They may very well be of two minds: they suspect him of criminal behaviour yet, because of the unusual circumstances, they may also be unsure. That may be one reason why they gave him police bail on such reasonable terms. And may I stress, Sir, that he is here today, having complied with the terms of that bail, and having given me very clear and very firm instructions to defend him on a plea of not guilty. The central issue is knowledge, and my client has told me what he told the police: he did not have any knowledge of the contents of the luggage and is determined to demonstrate this to the court at his trial.

The second point, Sir, is that this is a young man, a university student who, until a few days ago, had every expectation of continuing his studies until graduation. The trip to New York, he instructs me, was for the purpose of attending his sister's wedding, a fact that his father has confirmed to me. My client tells me he takes his studies seriously. During the past two years, he has consistently achieved at least 70% in all his papers, and this, Sir, is consistent with the profile of a diligent student rather than a drug trafficker. Although he is now acutely aware of the seriousness of the charge, and of the necessity of preparing for trial, he is still very anxious to complete his studies. As we are unlikely to obtain a trial date for at least seven to nine months, to detain him in custody or to provide bail conditions that are so onerous as to deprive him of his liberty is also to postpone an education he has obviously worked hard to get – not to mention the consequences of keeping him in a remand cell for many months with hardened criminals. This, I submit, would not be in his best interest and I sincerely doubt that the prosecution would want to see this result.

I shall conclude by proposing bail conditions that, hopefully, will satisfy this court that his attendance at trial is secured. First, he is prepared to report to the police every day, if necessary, and surrender his travel documents. Second, he will move out of his residence and live with his father at 9782 Highbury Road until trial. Third, his father has offered to stand surety in the amount of $50,000 and, if necessary, he can deposit that amount.

Unless I can be of further assistance, those are my submissions.

Outcome

After a few verbal exchanges, the magistrate fixed bail at $75,000 with the defendant's father standing surety for that amount and the defendant reporting to the police station daily.

Commentary

It is unusual for the police to give the defendant police bail on such a serious charge. By focusing on this fact, defence counsel was taking a gamble that the prosecution was not aware of the reason police bail was granted. Perhaps the reason was as defence counsel stated. Perhaps not. Perhaps it was just a lapse of judgment by the officer on duty, or a simple mistake. For defence counsel, the risk was that the prosecution could have asked for a short adjournment to try to discover why police bail was granted. But defence counsel, knowing that the prosecution is usually busy with a multitude of cases, gambled this would not occur. Defence counsel minimised the risk and avoided contentiousness by arguing the point as a mere hypothesis rather than as a fact. As defence counsel said: '[The police] *may* have seen this defendant as a very untypical defendant.' Coupled with the other facts, this was intended to plant a seed of doubt in the court's mind: 'The defendant was caught with drugs, Sir, but maybe something is going on under the surface that we don't know about. Maybe even the police have serious doubts about his guilt.'

An important lesson to learn here is not that defence counsel invariably gets lucky with police error, but that, when there is something weak about the prosecution's case or the way it has been handled, defence counsel needs to look for a way to make the most of it. Counsel did that here, but did not embrace the issue to the point of proclaiming the client's innocence. Counsel was still avoiding contentiousness and was being helpful to the court when she suggested reasonably stringent bail conditions – but not so stringent that they would prove a burden to her client.

Counsel was making a comprehensive offer, just as one might do in a negotiation, but an offer that was consistent with the argument. This is yet another example of helpfulness to the judge. Counsel suggested to the court what the terms of the bail order should be, being helpful in a way that would make it easy for the judge to make an order in her client's favour.

CHAPTER 3

PLEA IN MITIGATION

A plea in mitigation is a submission made by counsel to reduce the expected severity of the sentence. In the lower courts, where the judges have to deal with convicted criminals in such large numbers, defence counsel know that judges often have their minds made up about sentence before they hear from counsel. So, it is part of counsel's function to persuade the judge to hand down a sentence different from the one which the judge may already have decided upon.

Defence counsel should always be prepared to deliver a plea in mitigation no matter what the plea is. If the plea is guilty, the lawyer has to do everything possible to reduce the expected severity of the sentence, by negotiating with the prosecution and preparing and delivering an effective plea in mitigation. If the client's choice is to plead not guilty and try for an acquittal, the lawyer must also be prepared to deliver a plea in mitigation – in the event of a conviction.

THEORY OF THE CASE

All effective pleas in mitigation have the same purpose – to attract the greatest reduction in sentence, while at the same time ensuring that the sentence is still within the bounds of what is acceptable to the court. In the plea in mitigation, the advocate should balance getting the most for the client without pushing judges too far beyond their comfort zone. Judges view their role as guardians of the public welfare, responsible for ensuring that convicted persons get the outcome both they and the public deserve. Counsel needs to lead the judge gently to the outer limit of leniency, without threatening the judge's perception of that role.

Principles

As guardian of the public welfare, the judge has to consider three basic sentencing principles. Counsel should design the plea in mitigation based on these principles:

- deterrence of the public and the offender;
- rehabilitation of the offender;
- retribution.

A deterrent sentence is aimed at discouraging the public from committing the offence or the offender from offending again. A rehabilitative sentence is to assist the offender in learning new behaviour so he will not offend again. A retributive sentence is designed to express society's outrage against a particular offence.

When preparing the plea in mitigation, counsel has to know which principles (or combinations of principles) are appropriate. Although all three principles can be considered in deciding the sentence for many crimes, one principle will usually outweigh the others in judicial decision making. For example, with first time offenders who commit relatively trivial crimes, rehabilitation will usually weigh more heavily than deterrence. With more experienced offenders who commit serious crimes, deterrence of the offender will be most important. With first time offenders who commit very serious crimes, but are unlikely to do so again, the principle of retribution and, perhaps, deterrence of the public, will take precedence. (An example of this last type of case can be found in *R v Grabowski*, below, p 54).

SENTENCING APPROACHES

When preparing a plea, counsel has to take into account two sentencing approaches that the court will consider when sentencing. They are the *tariff* approach and the *individualised* approach. The tariff approach relies on objective standards of sentencing. Judges take this approach with more serious offences in which deterrence and retribution play a more important role than rehabilitation.

For less serious offences, the court will use an individualised approach, one that is more specifically tailored to the needs of the offender. In these cases, the court considers rehabilitation the main principle to be taken into account. When preparing the plea in mitigation, counsel must appreciate when to use which approach in a particular case.

The tariff approach

The court will adopt the tariff approach with certain common, serious offences such as robbery or drug trafficking where the principle of deterrence weighs heavily in judicial decision making.

When judges adopt the tariff approach, they employ a standard sentence (established by past sentencing of similar crimes) as a *starting point*. This starting point may be reduced or increased depending on whether there are *mitigating* or *aggravating* circumstances. For example, in a case of robbery where a knife is used as a threatening instrument, the starting point for a standard sentence may be seven years' imprisonment. *Mitigating* factors offered by counsel, such as a guilty plea, clear record or the youth of the offender, may reduce the sentence from the starting point. On the other hand, aggravating circumstances of the case, such as tying up the victims or cutting them with the knife, might add several years to the starting point.

When taking the tariff approach in a plea in mitigation, lawyers are saying that they accept that standard sentences apply and that the sentence will be based on objective standards laid down by the courts in tariff cases. Lawyers can find standard sentences for common offences handed down periodically by appeal courts in guideline judgments found in the law reports. These judgments, however, should not be viewed as cast in stone. Whenever possible, counsel should argue that the judgment should be adjusted to suit the specific circumstances of the client. Lawyers will find that, even when one argues for objective guidelines, there is usually some room to argue for an individualised approach, and for the sentence to be tailored to the client's circumstances.

The individualised approach and sentencing options

When aggravating circumstances are minimal, or when mitigating circumstances are strong enough so that rehabilitation outweighs deterrence or retribution, the argument can focus on ways to meet the offender's specific needs without undermining the role of the judge as guardian of the public welfare. This individualised approach to sentencing is usually appropriate when the offence is less serious and the offender is young, or a first time offender. It is also appropriate where circumstances indicate that there is a probability that the offender will not reoffend, or where it can be shown that imprisonment is unlikely to achieve positive results for the offender or society. In such cases, counsel can argue for a sentence to suit the specific circumstances of the offender and the offence. As a concept, the individualised approach does not exclude consideration of custodial sentences. Counsel can still argue for a shorter prison sentence because of the client's individual needs or circumstances. In practice, however, the individualised approach is usually associated with sentencing options other than imprisonment.

Frequently, a recommendation for an individualised sentence is made by a third party (usually a probation officer) in a *pre-sentence report*. After conviction and before sentence, the judge can adjourn the case, pending receipt of a pre-sentence report, which the judge can order when a decision needs to be made as to whether a defendant should go to prison or whether he is suitable for some other form of sentencing.

The pre-sentence report outlines the defendant's personal history, previous convictions, circumstances of the present offence, details of the defendant's response to, and insight about, his situation (usually based on an interview with the defendant), and a recommendation in relation to appropriate sentencing. When the report is completed, it is given to the court, the prosecution and defence counsel. Counsel should discuss the report with the client to ascertain to what extent he agrees with it.

The defendant then returns to court. Counsel delivers the plea in mitigation prior to sentencing. In the plea for an individualised sentence, counsel can agree with the report, suggest modifications to the recommendation, or dispute aspects of the report.

The judge will usually respond favourably to a plea to keep the defendant out of jail if it can be shown that the individualised arrangements suggested would reduce the likelihood that the defendant will repeat the offence. For example:

> Sir, it is clear, from the pre-sentence report, that the defendant's previous convictions are all alcohol related. This is the third time he has been caught in the middle of the night stealing or trying to steal automobile accessories. Each time, the thefts were committed with anything but stealth. Each time, he woke up the neighbourhood with his late-night bungling efforts. On this occasion, when the police appeared, he made no effort to run. He was still trying to pry the left rear hubcap off the vehicle when the first police constable on the scene told him he was under arrest. Each time, he was intoxicated and, according to what he told the probation officer, has no recollection of these incidents. It is clear that this defendant is suffering from a severe case of alcoholism and that he presents more of a danger to himself than to the public.

> In most cases, a third conviction for an offence such as this would probably mean prison. In this case, both the defendant and the public are likely to be best served if he can overcome his alcohol addiction. He has shown in the past that, when he is alcohol-free, he does not offend. I ask you to consider seriously the recommendation in the pre-sentence report that the defendant be put on probation for two years and that the main condition of his probation be that he attend a treatment programme at the Metrocity Substance Abuse Centre ...

In making the individualised sentence submission, counsel has access to a variety of sentencing options. It is up to counsel to suggest an option or combination of options that is appropriate to the client and the circumstances of the offence he has committed. Constrained by different rules and resources, various jurisdictions have different sentencing options, other than imprisonment. Some of those available in Metroland, for example, are set out below.

Suspended sentence

For certain offences, where a sentence of imprisonment is imposed, the sentence may be suspended in exceptional circumstances. If the defendant commits certain offences during the suspension, the court that can re-impose the original sentence of imprisonment.

Conditional or absolute discharge

Instead of imposing a sentence, the court can, with certain kinds of offences, grant an absolute or conditional discharge. With an absolute discharge, the defendant receives no punishment. With a conditional discharge, the defendant is discharged subject to committing no offences for a specific period.

Probation order

The offender's liberty is made subject to certain conditions that are supervised by a probation officer. These are often designed to address certain problems related to the defendant's criminal behaviour. Examples include attending an alcohol or drug treatment centre (as suggested above), residing or not residing in a particular place, refraining from associating with certain individuals or participating in certain activities, and reporting to the probation officer at appointed times.

Community service order

Under the supervision of a probation officer, the offender has to perform some community service for a fixed number of hours. Underlying community service is the idea that the offender is encouraged to develop a sense of social responsibility and compensate society for what he has done.

Fines

An order for payment of a fine is retributive and deterrent in purpose, but obviously not as severe as imprisonment. Defence counsel can suggest a fine in lieu of prison, arguing that prison might encourage contact with criminals and thus recidivism, while a fine will still punish without promoting a repetition of criminal behaviour.

In addition to these sentences, courts can also make ancillary orders, such as restitution of stolen property, compensation for personal injury, confiscation of profits from trafficking in illegal drugs and forfeiture of property used in the commission of a crime.

POINTS TO REMEMBER IN PREPARATION

Consulting higher authorities

To prepare for a plea in mitigation, lawyers should always consult two major sources: the first is experienced lawyers who have practised before the courts that are going to impose sentence on your client. The second is local sentencing authorities. Experienced lawyers will have fairly accurate perspectives on which sentencing principles apply, what the outer limits of leniency might be in particular circumstances and, perhaps most important, the attitudes of particular judges. Individual judges have special preferences or beliefs. Only experienced local practitioners who have practised in front of those judges can give reliable advice about how those judges might react to particular submissions.

In addition, local sentencing authorities are useful. These include local law reports, encyclopedias of sentencing that catalogue various crimes, and leading *sentencing guideline* cases. While consulting experienced lawyers and authorities is important in every aspect of law practice, it is critical in a plea in mitigation. If the courts consider an offence to be governed by a tariff and various degrees of imprisonment, it could be disastrous to adopt an individualised approach and ask for probation.

Aggravating and mitigating features

Counsel should always be aware of both the aggravating and mitigating features of the case. In most cases, aggravating features should not be ignored, but met head on. Ordinarily, counsel should acknowledge them to get them out of the way and show the judge they have not been forgotten. But then, as with any concession, they should immediately be counterbalanced with mitigating features or explanatory information. Here are two examples of how aggravating features are conceded, but then counterbalanced with mitigating ones:

- 'Your Honour, it is true that the defendant committed a breach of trust and this is undoubtedly the worst aspect of the case. But against this, I ask your Honour to consider that it was not greed, but intense financial pressure, that drove him to it – pressure that resulted from a chain of events that, as your Honour can see, was not wholly of his own making. He had a family to feed and a son to educate. I bring this to your Honour's attention not to suggest he has any excuse whatsoever for doing it, but rather to assist your Honour in understanding what moved him to do it ...'

- 'There is no question that the assault was brought on by drunkenness and that it caused injury. Fortunately for everyone, there was no permanent damage. The defendant feels extremely sorry for what he has done and, without being asked by Mr Falworth or his solicitor, paid compensation to him of $500. When the effects of the alcohol wore off, he co-operated completely with the police and pleaded guilty at the first available opportunity ...'

In some jurisdictions, both aggravating and mitigating features may have specific, quantifiable effects on the tariff. For example, an aggravating feature such as using a knife in a robbery can result in an automatic extension of a specific number of years to the duration of a prison sentence. Conversely, a mitigating feature such as the absence of a previous criminal record can result in a percentage discount in the length of the prison sentence. Where they exist, specific extensions and discounts can usually be found in guideline cases. Nevertheless, subject to limits imposed by statute, courts still have considerable flexibility in sentencing as they weigh aggravation against mitigation. That is why it is important, when preparing a plea in mitigation, to identify the key aggravating and mitigating factors in your case. The following is a list of some of the most commonly used.

Aggravating factors

1 Lack of remorse (eg, a plea of not guilty followed by a conviction)
2 Serious injury to victim
3 Extensive damage to or loss of property
4 Use of weapon
5 Vulnerability of victim (eg, young or elderly)
6 The defendant as ringleader
7 Previous convictions for similar offences
8 Committing offence while on bail
9 Unprovoked attack
10 Premeditated crime
11 Breach of trust

Mitigating factors

1 Show of remorse (eg, a plea of guilty)

2 No previous convictions

3 Youth

4 Little or no injury to persons or damage to property

5 Having made (rather than offered) restitution

6 Only a follower, not a ringleader

7 Provocation

8 Already suffered punishment (eg, job loss, injury)

9 Co-operated with police

10 Dependent children and/or spouse

11 Financial pressure not caused by defendant

Facts and previous convictions

Before the mitigation hearing, the prosecution will provide a statement of facts (or particulars of the offence) and a record of previous convictions. If the client disagrees with any of these, counsel should raise points of disagreement with the prosecution before the hearing. The prosecution will sometimes agree to omit facts prejudicial to the defendant, if the agreement is the outcome of a broader negotiation that results in the defendant pleading guilty and not putting the prosecution to the risk, expense and trouble of a full trial. Less frequently, where the defendant decides to plead guilty and there is disagreement about the facts that cannot be resolved through negotiations, the court can order a hearing be held to determine the facts. Where there are disagreements about convictions, the prosecution may be required to prove the disputed convictions.

STRUCTURE

The structure of the submission depends on the objective of the plea and whether the tariff or individualised approach is chosen. In the tariff approach, counsel still needs to address the defendant's individual circumstances. In the individualised approach, counsel should still pay attention to the standard sentences for that type of offence.

Structure of a plea in mitigation

1 Concede aggravating features of the case
2 Balance with theme of the case
3 Provide factual overview
4 Select approach (tariff or individualised)

For a tariff approach:

a identify appropriate sentencing principles
b identify appropriate authorities
c argue by analogy
d justify discounts
e adopt individualised approach

For an individualised approach:

a use effective theory to explain defendant's behaviour
b outline relevant mitigating factors consistent with theory
c present defendant's personal circumstances
d address the tariff, if appropriate
e suggest sentence appropriate to defendant's needs

For example, in a tariff-type plea, counsel might begin by conceding the most aggravating aspects of the case, but then balance this with the theme of the defendant's case or a concise summary of what counsel will argue, for example:

> There is no question that there was a lot cash taken, but I shall seek to persuade your Honour that the defendant's conduct needs first to be understood as the culmination of a sequence of unfortunate events, one piled on top of the other.

Then, counsel might provide a brief factual overview. This will not consist of all the facts, because some facts have already been dealt with in the prosecution's submission. It should include helpful facts not mentioned by the prosecution.

Counsel should then move on to identify the key tariff cases, argue by analogy and, based on the argument, justify discounts sought for the defendant.

Towards the end, counsel can move onto a more individualised approach, explaining (but not excusing) the defendant's behaviour, outlining mitigating factors, presenting personal circumstances, and outlining an appropriate sentence consistent with the defendant's needs, but within the limits of precedent.

With an individualised approach, there should be a greater emphasis on the theory of the defendant's behaviour and the defendant's personal circumstances so that counsel can suggest a sentence appropriate to the defendant's needs.

The following are two case studies. In the first, *R v Westgate*, counsel uses the individualised approach. In the second, *R v Grabowski*, counsel uses the tariff approach.

CASE STUDY 3: *R v WESTGATE*

Client's name: Charles Randall Westgate

Offence: Charge 1, Careless driving contrary to s 5 of the Motor Traffic Act [this reads in part: '(a) A person who drives a motor vehicle on a road carelessly commits an offence and is liable to a fine of $10,000 and a term of imprisonment not exceeding one year for a first offence; (b) A person drives carelessly within the meaning of this section if on a road he drives a vehicle without due care and attention or without reasonable consideration for other persons using the road.']

Charge 2, Driving with alcohol concentration above the prescribed limit contrary to s 9 of the Motor Traffic Act. [Maximum sentence is $100,000 and imprisonment for three years. Disqualification of the defendant's licence to drive for a period of not less than two years is mandatory in the case of a second or subsequent offence. Although a period of disqualification is not mandatory in the case of a first offence, the court has the power to disqualify the defendant under the provisions of s 18 of the Act. In Metroland, the practice is that drivers are normally disqualified for a first offence for 12–18 months unless exceptional circumstances can be shown.]

Particulars alleged by the prosecution (and agreed by the defendant)

On the morning of 2 May Yr0 at approximately 4.45 am, at the junction of Cordery Road and Naismith Street, a green delivery van with commercial markings and licence number 7SP 2W5 crashed into a stationary vehicle with licence number 900 6G4 parked at the above location. This vehicle was severely damaged in the rear.

The green delivery van was also seriously damaged in the front. PC 70427 arrived at the scene of the accident and observed the defendant at the wheel of his car apparently dazed. He appeared uninjured, but was observed mumbling to himself. When asked what he was doing in a delivery van in the middle of the night, the defendant answered that he owned the van and was driving to see his sick mother. After checking his licence and registration the PC conducted a breathalyser reading and recorded 86 micrograms in 100 millilitres of breath. The prescribed limit is 35 micrograms.

The defendant was taken to Metroland Central Police station where he was given another breathalyser, which resulted in a reading of 74 micrograms in 100 millilitres of breath.

Client's address: 6831 Kenilworth Crescent.

Age and marital status: 54. Divorced and remarried, he has one daughter from his second marriage, age 10. He has two grown children from his first marriage.

Employment and income: Defendant has been working as an independent contractor making deliveries for a variety of companies for the past 14 years. He has a hire purchase contract on his van. The contract stipulates that he has to pay off the van with 12 instalments of $600 a month. He intends to pay this off by the end of the current year.

Previous convictions: Yr–28 (age 25), common assault. This is unrelated and in any event should be treated as spent. Defendant has had a driving licence for 24 years. He has a clear driving record.

Personal and other particulars (notes prepared by defendant's solicitors)

Mr Westgate was asleep when he was woken by a telephone call from his 76 year old mother at about 4 am on Sunday. Suffering from liver problems for several years, his mother was having a painful attack. She asked him to come over immediately. She lived alone and was fearful this might be the end. Client hung up and called an ambulance, and was told it could take as long as 20 minutes. His mother lived about 10 minutes away by car in an apartment complex called Glen Gardens. He dressed quickly and ran out to his van. It was raining and the roads were slippery. He sped along Cordery Road, and nearing Naismith he swerved to avoid a dog crossing the street, lost control and collided with a parked vehicle on Cordery Road.

Earlier, that Saturday afternoon, Mr Westgate entertained his brother and family at the client's home. Mr Westgate said he drank about four cans of beer. After dinner, he shared a bottle of wine with his wife and fell asleep watching television sometime after midnight. When he received the call from his mother, he remembered he had been drinking but he thought he could not be over the limit. He had not had the wine on an empty stomach and assumed the effects of alcohol had worn off. He was very concerned about his mother. He thought he would reach her house before the ambulance arrived so he could comfort her and accompany her to the hospital. He did not call a taxi because at that late hour it would have taken at least 30 minutes for the taxi to arrive.

Because of his job as a driver, client says he only drinks on Saturdays and Sundays. When he comes home Saturday morning after his last delivery of the week, he hangs up his keys, doesn't drive and relaxes around the house. His wife drives at the weekends.

Since 2 May Yr0, client has been on police suspension unable to drive his van and having to sub-contract out his work to another company. The plea is fixed to be heard on 29 May. Client did not consider a not guilty plea, nor would he instruct me to investigate the strength of his case on a not guilty plea. Client's van is still in the shop for repairs and will be there until the end of June owing to a parts shortage. His largest contract is with a newspaper, the Metrocity Sun-Times. His wife is a part time cashier at Ranier's Supermarket. During this period they are going to have to live off savings and borrow money from his wife's mother. He arranged for his insurance to pay for the damage to the parked vehicle, but for his van he will have to pay all of the damages amounting to approximately $4,000.

Prosecution's position

The prosecution takes no position but expects a fine of $1,000 on the first charge and a licence suspension of at least one year on the second charge.

Lawyer's strategy

- The usual penalty on the second charge of impaired driving is at least one year's licence suspension. In order to attract something lower than that I have to demonstrate 'exceptional circumstances' under s 7 of the Act. In such a case, the court does have a discretion, but does not often exercise it.

- A professional van driver with a conviction for impaired driving is not the kind of person in whose favour the court would want to exercise discretion. Judges take their responsibilities seriously and the fact that he is a delivery van driver means he is constantly on the road. This judge could well have visions of mangled pedestrians in his head and newspaper headlines blaming the judge for putting a 'drunk' back on the road in his delivery van. And yet, what my client desperately needs is to go back to work as quickly as possible, otherwise he might permanently lose all his contracts and end up impoverished.

- I should start with the aggravating features – the extensive damage to the vehicles and the fact that, being aware he had been drinking, he still took a serious risk by driving.

- I want to get these out of the way first so that I can concentrate on the exceptional, mitigating circumstances. I want to show that this case is different from the usual impaired driving cases. I will point out that the purpose of his driving that night, if not admirable, was at least well intentioned. He wasn't out drinking with his friends, subsequently deciding recklessly to drive home. He was not out on a date showing off in front of his girlfriend. He was not an alcoholic whose breathalyser reading is always over the limit. He was a middle aged man roused in the middle of the night by an emergency call from his mother. With little alternative, he left the house to go to his mother's with the intention of saving her life. The offence also occurred in the early morning hours of the morning when hardly anyone was on the road.
- Of course, there are other mitigating features and I will discuss those too, but it is the uniqueness of the case that I need to get across. If the court seems inclined to leniency I may even try to get a very brief period of suspension.

Oral submission

Defence counsel: Sir, I appear on behalf of the defendant. My client is ready to
(Ms Calhoun)   plead.

[*1st charge is read to the defendant.*]

Defence counsel: How do you plead?

Defendant: Guilty.

[*2nd charge is read to the defendant.*]

How do you plead?

Defendant: Guilty.

[*The prosecution reads aloud the particulars of the offence as previously agreed between her and defence counsel.*]

Magistrate: Do you admit to the facts on both charges?

Defendant: Yes.

Magistrate: Upon your plea of guilty and admission of the facts I convict on both charges. Counsel, any mitigation?

Defence counsel: Sir, I am grateful.

There may be one or two aspects of this case that might cause you concern. It is true that two vehicles including my client's were damaged and that he was driving over the prescribed limit. But there is more to the story than that.

This is a very unique case – so much so that I shall seek to persuade you, Sir, that there are exceptional circumstances and that any licence suspension you may see fit to impose on the second charge should be much shorter than is usually the case in this court.

Permit me then, Sir, to explain briefly the background to the events leading up to the accident.

The defendant drives a delivery van for various companies in the Metrocity area. His main employer is The Metrocity Sun-Times, although he has been engaged in this work as an independent contractor for the past 14 years. He drives all week, and at weekends it is his unvarying habit not to drive. He hangs up his keys on Saturday morning after his last delivery with no intention of driving until he returns to work early Monday morning. When transport is needed at the weekend, his wife drives.

There was no reason to depart from this practice on the weekend of the accident. My client was relaxing at home with his wife and 10 year old daughter that Saturday. They had a barbecue lunch with my client's brother and family. My client recalls consuming around four cans of beer. After his brother left, my client and his wife had a late dinner that ended at about half past nine. After dinner, he and his wife shared a bottle of white wine. He fell asleep while watching television sometime after midnight.

At around 4 am on Sunday, he was woken up by a telephone call from his 76 year old mother, who lives 10 minutes away in an apartment complex called Glen Gardens. She has recently been suffering from liver problems. She was in pain and in a highly distressed state. Living alone, she feared the worst. She asked my client to come over immediately. And, Sir, he did so. His purpose was, of course, to help her. His statement to the police constable who came on the scene a little later corroborated that purpose. The PC reported that my client said he was on his way to see his sick mother. My instructions are that his mind was completely focused on reaching his mother's home as soon as possible. He did not have time to give much thought to his ability to drive. Nor, when he did think about it, did he think his ability to drive would be affected by the alcohol he consumed the night before. He assumed, wrongly it turned out, that the effects of the alcohol he had consumed the night before would have already worn off.

Magistrate: Why didn't he call an ambulance? Surely that would have been a more sensible solution?

Defence counsel: In fact, Sir, he did, but was told the ambulance could take up to 20 minutes. At this point, he felt he had to make his way to her home as soon as he possibly could. Sir, he also considered calling a taxi, but knew at that hour of the morning it could take up to 30 minutes.

There is no denying that he did have options. He could have waited for a taxi. He could have let the ambulance handle it. He could have woken his wife, asked her to drive and taken his sleeping daughter into the van – had he thought he had enough time. But, Sir, this was a high-stress moment for my client. To his mind, his mother was in grave danger at 4 o'clock in the morning and needed his help. His behaviour was not excusable, and it was not lawful but, I submit, it was understandable.

It is certainly different from the typical case. This is not a case of a habitual drinking driver. This is not a case where someone goes out with friends for a few drinks and who then, despite being under the influence, deliberately or recklessly takes the risk of driving home, hoping not to get caught or, indeed, not even bothering to think of the risks. This is a case, I submit, where there are, to use the words of the statute, 'exceptional circumstances'.

Having submitted that, Sir, I would be grateful if I could briefly outline further relevant mitigating factors and my client's financial situation.

First, the mitigating factors:

My client accepts fully that he did take a serious risk.

He did plead guilty at the first available opportunity.

May I also stress, Sir, that no one was injured. My client instructs me that he swerved to avoid hitting a dog, and that was the immediate cause of the accident. There was damage to the parked vehicle, but my client has already made arrangements through his insurer to pay the costs of the repairs to the owner of the car.

My client has been driving for over 24 years and has a clean driving record, which I am sure you will agree is exemplary.

Sir, my client's financial situation: he is an independent contractor, and as a result of the accident he has been unable to work, as his van requires substantial repairs. He does, however, remain obligated to pay the sum of $600 per month to cover the hire purchase instalments. Although his wife works part time as a cashier, the family of three still requires his contribution, especially to meet the child's education costs. This unfortunate situation has already cost my client a great deal of money that he cannot afford. He has to cover the cost of repairing his own van, which will be in the neighbourhood of $4,000 and, not being eligible for legal aid, he does have legal fees as well. With that in mind, I urge you to consider a small fine on the first charge, say $500, to be paid in instalments if possible.

In relation to the period of suspension, clearly any period of suspension would seriously affect the defendant's livelihood. He has been employed as a driver for the past 14 years and it is unlikely that he is qualified to perform any other jobs other than menial tasks at low pay.

Magistrate: How long will his van be in the shop for repairs?

Defence counsel: Sir, it has already been in the shop since 2 May. That is nearly four weeks. It is estimated it will need another four weeks. Apparently there is a parts shortage.

Sir, your inquiry leads me to my final submission. I urge you to take into account that the defendant has been under police suspension since the date of the accident, nearly a month ago. He is licensed to drive only that van. I urge you to consider that that any suspension period you may have in mind cover the period the van is being repaired, that is four more weeks. That will make the suspension approximately eight weeks in all – two months. If it is much longer than that, my client fears he will lose his contracts to other providers and he will be without any income whatsoever.

As such, Sir, I am requesting a period of suspension on the second charge of four weeks from today.

Unless I can assist you further, those are my submissions.

Outcome

Magistrate: Thank you, counsel. There will be a six week suspension on the second charge. The expiry date is 13 July, Yr0. He can drive again on 14 July. On the first charge, there will be a fine of $1,000. Mr Westgate?

Defendant: Yes, Sir?

Magistrate: In line with counsel's submissions, I have found there are exceptional circumstances in your case and that, therefore, the period of suspension should be considerably shorter than usual. Nevertheless, I am not impressed with your conduct. Driving while under the influence of alcohol is one of the most serious crimes that come through this court. I see it every single day and I see the death, injury and destruction it causes. So you are very fortunate to get off so lightly today, Mr Westgate. Should you ever appear in this court again on a similar charge, this court will not listen to a plea of 'exceptional circumstances'. You will definitely go to prison for a long time. And no appeal by your lawyer or your family will keep you out of prison. Do you understand?

Defendant: Yes.

Defence counsel: Time to pay, Sir?

Magistrate: How long do you need in order to pay the fine, Mr Westgate?

Defendant: Three months, Sir?

Magistrate: I'll give you a little longer than that. Payment to be made on or before 10 September, Yr0.

Commentary

In this individualised approach to mitigation, counsel achieved what her client needed. Westgate needed to get back on the road to earn a living and counsel persuaded the court that this was the right outcome. As with any individualised mitigation, counsel's purpose is to demonstrate that her client's case is different and that the sentence should be different in a way that suits the client's needs.

The argument also meets the criteria of emotional and logical appeal discussed in Chapter 1. For emotional appeal, counsel's argument was like the defence of necessity. Her client had to get in his vehicle and drive in order to save his mother. Granted, this was somewhat melodramatic, but it was the most obvious explanation for his behaviour. As for logical appeal, counsel demonstrated how the facts fit 'exceptional circumstances'. She contrasted her client's virtuous motivation with the much more common case of someone who goes out drinking with his friends and makes the reckless decision to drive home.

To avoid contentiousness, counsel conceded that what her client did was 'not excusable and not lawful', but it was 'understandable'. For her client to drive his car when over the prescribed limit was not justifiable, but there was an explanation and counsel gave it. To ensure the explanation was believable and not concocted later, counsel focused on the facts, reminding the magistrate that the defendant at the scene of the accident did tell the police constable that he was going to see his sick mother. What he said to the police constable then and what he was saying in court now were consistent. On this issue, however, counsel might have prepared more thoroughly by producing a hospital or ambulance record showing that her client's mother was admitted to hospital on the morning of 2 May.

To a considerable degree, counsel also followed the submission structure outlined above, p 45. She began by conceding the aggravating features of the case, went on to suggest her theory of the case to explain the defendant's behaviour, outlined mitigating factors, presented his personal circumstances and suggested a sentence appropriate to his needs.

CASE STUDY 4: *R v GRABOWSKI*

Client's name: Michael Beryl Grabowski

Offence: Causing death by dangerous driving, s 3 of the Motor Traffic Act [maximum prison sentence is 10 years with a one year minimum driving licence disqualification].

Particulars alleged by prosecution (and agreed by the defendant)

On 18 March Yr0, at approximately midnight, the defendant, Grabowski, age 22, left home in his motor vehicle. He had just had a lengthy argument with his parents over their disapproval of his plan to marry his girlfriend, who is pregnant. The defendant had no particular destination in mind when he left home, but he was in an angry mood when he got into his car. He headed north on to Queensborough Parkway driving at high speed. The victim, a 23 year old woman, had just completed her evening shift as a desk clerk at a nearby hotel, and was crossing Queensborough Parkway at the corner of Paxton Ferry Road with two friends from work. At that corner, there is a traffic light that flashes green indicating that both north and southbound traffic on Queensborough can proceed, but with caution. There is also a pedestrian-controlled light enabling pedestrians to cross Queensborough. This is activated by pushing a button on the traffic light pole, after which the traffic light for Queensborough traffic will turn yellow and then red. Queensborough is a brightly lit road, but visibility to pedestrians crossing at Paxton Ferry Road, looking south, is not especially good because, when crossing, pedestrians are just below the summit of a hill and need to stretch to see over it in order to catch sight of northbound traffic. The speed limit in the area is 30 miles per hour. The victim and her friends did not activate the pedestrian light because, when they were about to cross, they did not see any traffic approaching from either the south or the north.

As they walked across Queensborough, the victim was struck by the defendant's car and she suffered fatal head injuries from which she died in hospital several hours later. The defendant claimed he did not see the victim until it was too late. He applied his brakes and swerved to the right but struck the victim with the left front fender. There was no indication he had been drinking. Eyewitnesses estimated that the defendant was driving at approximately 60–70 miles per hour. The police have witnesses at the accident scene and at a location about 500 metres south on Queensborough who provided these estimates. Although the defendant denied to the police he was going that fast, he did admit to driving at about 55 miles per hour for 'some distance up Queensborough'. For the purposes of this hearing, the following was agreed: when he struck the victim he was going 55–60 miles per hour and that for about 500 yards prior to reaching Paxton Ferry Road, he was driving, at times, up to a speed of 60 miles per hour. It was also agreed that, other than driving in excess of the speed limit, he did not otherwise breach any traffic signals or signs. He was very upset and expressed remorse to the police, admitting that he should have been paying attention to his driving instead of being distracted by his anger toward his parents.

Client's address: 5982 Bainbridge Crescent, Ocean City. Lives with his parents, both of whom have retired. He is the youngest of three children. The first two have moved out and have families of their own.

Age and marital status: 22, single.

Employment and income: Defendant graduated from Hillcrest Technical College in June, Yr–1, having received a diploma in software programming. Since that time, he has worked as a software analyst trainee for Delford Communications Ltd, where he earns $2,000 per month.

Previous convictions: None. Clear driving record.

Personal and other particulars (notes prepared by defendant's solicitors)

Grabowski did not have a good relationship with his parents. They put too much pressure on him to continue his education. They wanted him to enrol at University and try to obtain a degree in computer science. When he told them his girlfriend was pregnant and that he wanted to marry her, they thought his chances of continuing his education would be ruined. When he left the house that night he was very angry and felt like driving fast, which is something he had done before without incident. As far as he was concerned, the light at the corner of Paxton Ferry Road was green and he had the right to proceed through it. He felt that, if the victim had used the pedestrian light, she would probably still be alive. Although he apparently blames the victim, he also feels very remorseful and is still shocked and incredulous at what has occurred.

This is Grabowski's first encounter with the law. He is terrified of spending time in prison, but has been advised that prison is almost a certainty. He will plead guilty.

Prosecution's position

The prosecution has said that it will take no position on the length of the prison term, but expects a sentence in excess of 18 months. They will cite the Guideline case, several supporting cases and will describe one aggravating feature of the case – the fact that the defendant was speeding along Queensborough Parkway for some considerable distance. [Prosecution and defence agreed to a licence disqualification of three years.]

Lawyer's strategy

- This is a tariff case with not much leeway for an individualised approach. I do not think I can keep him out of prison and, even if I am fortunate enough to do so, the prosecution will almost certainly appeal. The government takes a dim view of this kind of offence and only recently raised the maximum penalty from five to 10 years. Relatives of traffic victims are understandably devastated and outraged by the senseless deaths of loved ones. The relatives of the victim may be in court that day. I am going to try to ask for the most lenient prison sentence possible, but not so lenient as to unnerve the judge or (if she accepts my submissions) provoke the prosecution into an appeal. Unless the judge asks me, I will not raise two factual points: the first concerns the victim's own role in the accident, the second concerns the defendant's 'reasons' for speeding.

- In relation to the victim's role in the accident, it is undoubtedly true that she might have been saved had she used the pedestrian light. She was careless to a certain degree in not using it. But the law does not require her to use it and the flashing green light communicates to drivers along Queensborough that they must proceed with caution. Since the speed limit was 30, and since it was night time, the defendant should have slowed down to a speed of less than 30. Yet, he was going at least 55 miles per hour at the time of impact. He did not even brake until impact, because he did not see the victim at all. Putting any of the blame – even the smallest part – on the victim is too risky, likely to be too contentious. After all, a young woman is dead as a result of my client's behaviour. Besides, I am sure the judge is fully aware of the facts. It will probably be much more effective to leave this point untouched – to demonstrate my client's acceptance of responsibility.

- The second point is the 'reasons' for my client's speeding, his anger with his parents: I do not believe this should be mentioned, except peripherally. It is no excuse; it is not even an appropriate explanation for his behaviour. It is just his immaturity. On the other hand, one could say that since the accident – indeed, because of it – Grabowski has matured quite a bit. His life will never be the same.

- The Guideline case is *Boswell* (1984) 6 Cr App R(S) 227, which sets out the various aggravating and mitigating factors. Aggravating factors include one that my client is guilty of – excessive speed carried on for a distance. Mitigating factors include a good driving record, good character, a plea of guilty, and the defendant's reaction to the event – upset, shock and remorse.

- As long as an aggravating feature exists, I shall have to look to the guidelines, suggest that this feature is relatively minor, and demonstrate that the client should be near the bottom end of the sentencing scale.

Oral submission

[The prosecution made a brief submission, outlining the facts, the principles in the *Boswell* case, some supporting cases and the aggravating feature – excessive speed carried on for a distance.]

Defence counsel: If it please your Honour, the defendant accepts that this is a
(Ms Marchand) very serious offence with the most tragic consequences imaginable. As a result, he is still in shock and deeply remorseful for what he has done, as well as for the grief he has caused Miss Pettit's family. Your Honour, he knows he will have to go to prison. The issue we need to deal with today is to determine how long his sentence should be. As my learned friend has pointed out, sentences generally range from a month or two, where aggravating features are minimal, to several years where there are serious aggravating circumstances – for example, drunk driving, racing, disregard of warnings from passengers, several people killed. As in *Boswell*, your Honour needs to look at the aggravating and mitigating features of the offence, weigh them and decide where this case should rest on the scale. I shall seek to persuade your Honour that it should fall on the lower – perhaps lowest – end of the scale.

As my learned friend has also explained, *Boswell* sets out those matters that may be regarded as aggravating features. The prosecution has suggested that there is such a feature in this case – excessive speed carried on for a distance leading up to the collision.

This feature needs to be looked at carefully in the context of other similar cases.

Your Honour, I propose to discuss three such cases – all Court of Appeal decisions – to assist your Honour in this comparison. They have several features in common with the case at bar. All three involve a conviction on the charge of causing death by dangerous driving. All three defendants were young men in their 20s. No drinking was involved in any of the cases and all three were previously of good character. In all three cases, the aggravating feature was excessive speed.

If your Honour would be kind enough to look at the first case, *Attorney General's Reference No 3 of 1997 (Sean Lesley Bramley)* (1997) Volume 2, Criminal Appeal Reports (Sentencing) p 336 – at tab 3, your Honour. This was quite a serious case of excessive speed on a carriageway. The defendant, Bramley, was driving at a speed of between 96 and 106 miles per hour on a carriageway where the speed limit was 60 and then 70 miles per hour. There were warning signs on the carriageway that a junction was approaching. It appears from the facts, your Honour, that the defendant was observed driving at an excessive speed – in excess of 90 miles per hour for more than a mile – prior to the collision. He was driving so fast that, even after he saw the victims' vehicle and collided with the victims' car, his speed was estimated at 85 miles per hour. In the car that he struck was a family of four. The father and child were killed and the mother and another child were seriously injured.

If I can bring your Honour to p 338, down to the second-to-last paragraph. As Mr Justice Rose concludes, 'It was an even greater tragedy for the family who lost two of its members, one of them a child. The speed was very great. The car had been driven at a considerable speed over a significant stretch of highway'. On this Appeal, your Honour, the defendant's sentence was raised from 12 months to two years.

I should point out to your Honour that Bramley pleaded not guilty and there was a jury trial.

The next case, your Honour, is *Attorney General's Reference Nos 17 and 18 of 1996 (Mark Andrew Iseton and Lee Wardle)* (1997) Volume 1, Criminal Appeal Reports (Sentencing) p 247 – at tab

4, your Honour. In this case, there were two defendants, Iseton and Wardle, Wardle being the one I shall focus on. The two defendants were driving separate cars and did not know each other. In a 30 mile an hour zone, they stopped at a red light. When the light turned green, Iseton accelerated to 60 miles per hour and Wardle followed close behind. They drove this way for about a third of a mile. Iseton, too late, saw a pedestrian crossing the road, and swerved to avoid her. Wardle, following close behind, braked hard and swerved to the right, colliding with the pedestrian and killing her. Wardle pleaded not guilty and was convicted at trial with a sentence of 12 months' imprisonment. On appeal, the Court of Appeal said the sentence should have been 21 months, but they declined to impose it because Wardle only had a week or two to serve on his original sentence.

As in the case at bar, Wardle pleaded guilty, but one important point of comparison needs to be drawn: although Wardle and Iseton were not found to have been racing, they were driving too close together in what appeared to be a deliberate manner. In my submission, compared to the defendant in this case, Wardle's conduct added an extra layer of danger to the act of speeding. By deliberately driving so fast and so close behind Iseton for such a distance, he was reducing his field of vision and his ability to manoeuvre. This was reflected in his sentence.

The last case to which I invite your Honour to refer is *Simon Carr* (1996) Volume 1, Criminal Appeal Reports (Sentencing) p 107 – at tab 5, your Honour. Carr was on a motorway at about 1.30 am and driving for a considerable distance at a speed faster than 80 miles per hour. At one point, according to police, he was going about 90 miles per hour. He slammed into another vehicle whose driver, a young woman, died as a result. The defendant was driving at such a speed that he carried on for another 175 metres after impact, at one point climbing over an embankment at the side of the motorway. The defendant said at trial he did not see the driver because 'he nodded off momentarily'. The learned trial judge instructed the jury that if he had momentarily fallen asleep, he would not be guilty of dangerous driving. The fact that the jury found him guilty was reason enough for the learned trial judge to conclude that they did not accept his evidence on this point. He went on to refer to the fact that the defendant had been driving at high speed for some distance. His sentence was six months, and this was upheld on appeal.

Your Honour, to recapitulate: Bramley was driving at very high speed for at least a mile. Two people died and two were seriously injured. Thus, in addition to speeding, there was the aggravating feature of multiple deaths. Bramley also did not plead guilty. He received two years. Wardle would have received 21 months, and he was engaged in deliberate and dangerous conduct *in addition to* speeding. He pleaded guilty. In those two cases, there was an aggravating feature in addition to speeding. In *Carr*, there was just excessive speed, albeit carried on for a distance. Carr received six months. The facts in the case at bar, I submit, are probably closest to *Carr*. In both, there is only one aggravating feature – excessive speed carried on for a distance.

Your Honour, on the other side of the coin, there are mitigating features. The defendant is of good character, has never been in trouble, has not even received a traffic ticket. He graduated from Hillcrest Technical College last year and since that time has been working for Delford Communications, training there as a software analyst. He would have had a good career ahead of him but for this tragedy. As your Honour can see, the letter from his employer speaks highly of him and his prospects. Nonetheless, prison will mean the loss of his job with no commitment by his employer to rehire him when he gets out of prison. Whatever punishment is handed out to him will be compounded by this loss.

Keeping in mind the six month sentence in *Carr*, the most important point I would like to make in concluding is this: I have talked with the defendant at length; he has shown deep remorse as well as great sorrow for what he has done. If his conduct was the result of immaturity – which I am sure it was – then, since the accident, he has grown up at a speed and to a degree that he could not have possibly imagined beforehand. In no way since the tragedy has he tried to evade responsibility or to minimise his role in it. Whatever the length of his custodial sentence, your Honour, it will be sufficient to bring home to him the enormity of the tragedy.

If I may, your Honour, I'd like to suggest that, unlike Carr, who pleaded not guilty and went to trial, this defendant pleaded guilty at the first opportunity and has not wavered in his intention to accept his punishment. In doing so, he has spared the victim's family the necessity of reliving in a trial the trauma they have already suffered. He has also spared them the delay and uncertainty that a trial would bring. For these reasons, your Honour, I submit that, as compared with *Carr*, this defendant merits a significant discount. I submit that an appropriate sentence might be in the range of two to four months.

Unless I can assist your Honour further, those are my submissions.

Outcome

Although it agreed with counsel that Grabowski, unlike Carr, merited a significant discount for pleading guilty, the court said that, in allowing his anger to direct his driving, Grabowski's conduct merited greater censure. Young people had to learn that driving demanded the highest degree of self-control, that motor vehicles were no different from dangerous weapons in that respect. The court determined that Grabowski's conduct was of a sufficiently aggravating character to balance the benefits of his guilty plea. Accordingly, his sentence should be nearly the same as Carr's. The judge handed down a sentence of five months' imprisonment.

Commentary

Counsel's argument is typical of the tariff approach to mitigation. It is precedent-based legal argument. A precedent-based legal argument uses objective legal standards based on precedents to justify a position taken in argument. It uses reasoning by similarity (or analogy): the closer the precedent's facts are to the facts of the case being argued, the more persuasive is the judgment expressed in that precedent. By focusing on the facts, counsel was able to argue that, of the three cases, *Carr* was the most similar to *Grabowski* and, therefore, Grabowski's sentence should be closest to Carr's.

In relation to tariff offences, the State has a strong deterrent or punitive policy. No matter how sympathetic judges might feel toward defendants and how effective defence counsel is, the court must sentence according to objective standards. In tariff cases, rehabilitative considerations are generally minimal. These are crimes that the State regards as so serious, that creating sympathy for the wrongdoer will rarely keep the offender out of jail.

An effort to create too much sympathy for the offender can arouse contentiousness. It can backfire, demonstrating to the judge that the offender may still be unable to take responsibility for his crime. In a case of causing death by dangerous driving, defence counsel needs to be acutely aware of this dynamic as well as the public pressure on the judge. The family of the victim may be sitting in court still overwhelmed by the tragedy that has befallen them. Defence counsel, therefore, must choose her words carefully in a way that avoids too great an emotional appeal on behalf of the client. As an approach to argument, reasoning by similarity is perfect in this respect because it relies on cold, hard facts and law – on logical appeal rather than the stirring of emotions in a bid for sympathy.

This, however, does not mean that, when the tariff approach is appropriate, the individualised approach is abandoned. In sentencing, the court always has some discretion, the defendant is always a unique individual and defence counsel always has some scope for an individualised approach, particularly towards the end of the plea when counsel has completed her argument by similarity. In this case, the defendant was individualised at the end of the submission when counsel distinguished her client from *Carr*, and referred to specific mitigating factors such as her client's age, remorse and plea of guilty. Counsel was saying that her client's immaturity was at the root of his crime, but he had now accepted responsibility and by doing so had saved the victim's family from further trauma; *any* prison sentence would make him grow up in a hurry. This carried a subtle emotional appeal rather than an overt one. Counsel implied that her client had already suffered greatly from a tragedy that would change his life forever.

Some lawyers, in some jurisdictions, however, might have taken a more cold blooded, mathematical approach, because in some jurisdictions both age and a guilty plea are mitigating factors which support a percentage discount in sentence. So, for example, in such a jurisdiction, counsel could argue that the defendant's guilty plea and his obvious remorse could attract as much as a 30% discount in his sentence. Thirty per cent of Carr's six months is almost two months. If the 30% rule applied in Metroland, counsel could have argued the sentence be reduced to four months on this basis.

Why didn't Grabowski's lawyer argue for a non-custodial sentence? The answer to this question highlights the essence of effective mitigation in a tariff-type case. Counsel's goal is to reduce the degree of punishment as much as possible, but within the bounds of precedent. Counsel can achieve this best by helping the judge to grasp the logical means by which the sentence can be reduced without stretching the reduction beyond what society will perceive as fair. Here again, counsel is a helper, leading the judge gently, but systematically, through similar precedents. She does not make a leap into contentious territory by suggesting that the client stay out of prison altogether. If she had done so, she might have undermined her function as a helper, a guide on whom the judge could rely. In this case, counsel felt that, on the strength of the precedents, she did not have a chance at a non-custodial sentence. So she showed the judge how a brief prison sentence could be justified.

CHAPTER 4

THE CIVIL LITIGATION PROCESS AND NON-TRIAL ADVOCACY

In civil non-trial advocacy, lawyers can make a variety of pre-trial applications to court. In some jurisdictions, these applications are called interlocutory applications or interlocutory summonses. In others, they are called motions, chambers applications, or pre-trial applications. In Metroland, they are referred to as *interim applications*. These applications ordinarily take longer to prepare, requiring more analysis of fact and more precise and detailed advocacy than criminal applications. They also generally involve more documentation, particularly written evidence in the form of affidavits.

The three civil case studies in Chapters 5, 6 and 7 illustrate a variety of legal skills used in making interim applications to court. To benefit fully from the case studies, readers should familiarise themselves with the civil procedure of their jurisdiction and the role of the interim application in it. This chapter provides an introduction to this topic, briefly examining the following:

- the civil justice system;
- the civil litigation process;
- preparation of interim applications;
- presentation of interim applications.

THE CIVIL JUSTICE SYSTEM

People seek the advice of lawyers when they are in conflict with someone. They feel wronged, unjustly accused of committing a wrong, or they know they have done wrong and want to minimise their liability. They want a just solution to their problem. Lawyers are supposed to solve their problem and see that justice is done at minimal cost.

The character of the legal system is adversarial. One party fights the other for justice. When lawyers are retained, it is they who put together the case for each party, investigating, planning, organising and communicating so that the court can make sense of the parties' claims and defences. The judge plays a relatively passive role, deciding the outcome based on the evidence presented. The system calls for competent advocates to uphold their client's interests to the best of their ability. When competent advocates fulfil this duty, matching wits with each other in and out of court, the theory is that justice will ultimately prevail.

Critics of the system point out, however, that when one or both sides pull out all legal stops to win, or when one side has more resources than the other, achieving justice can take a long time. It can also be very expensive and complicated. Lord Woolf's review of the civil justice system and the subsequent passage of the Civil Procedure Rules 1998 (CPR) in England have attempted to address some of the excesses of the adversarial system – unfairness, tactical exploitation and inefficiency. These rules are too wide ranging and complex to discuss in detail here. I refer readers to the excellent texts that explain them, their practical uses and the background to their development.[1] Nevertheless, a few fundamental points about the CPR should be stressed, because they shed light on how the adversarial system has been modified and how this affects the way lawyers plan and prepare their cases and interim applications.

The CPR have the overriding objective of enabling the courts to deal with cases justly (CPR r 1.1(1)). This objective is met in a variety of ways. One of them is in the modification of the role of judges, so that they adopt a more active, rather than passive approach to case management. The CPR shifted the control of costs and the time scale of cases from litigants and their lawyers to the judges. The CPR achieved this through instituting a system of case management in which simple cases are channelled into standard litigation routines, while complex cases, requiring active and flexible management, are channelled to the courts. This way, litigants are less able to use manoeuvring tactics that use up both the opposition's and the court's resources.

Another innovative feature of the CPR is the concept of proportionality: amounts spent in bringing civil actions or in defending them should be proportionate to the amount involved in the litigation. Some reports suggest that the CPR are already resulting in fewer legal actions, faster settlements and fewer resource wasting interim applications.

The CPR give judges greater control over the kinds of manoeuvres lawyers make, even the kinds of interim applications they bring and defend. Under its mandate of 'dealing with cases justly', the court now has broader powers than it ever did to decide interim applications on the merits, override technical objections and make immediate awards of costs in fixed amounts against those who act unreasonably. This could reduce obstructive tactics and increase co-operation between the parties. By enabling judges to make immediate awards of costs, the CPR may be able to discourage lawyers from bringing weak interim applications to court or putting up weak defences to them.

Unlike the previous set of rules, the CPR explicitly recognise that litigation is expensive and that it should be avoided wherever possible. This has prompted the creation of systems to encourage settlement in the early stages

---

1   In the Bibliography, four books are listed: Plant, C (ed), *Blackstone's Civil Practice 2000*; May, A (LJ) (ed), *Civil Procedure (The White Book Service 2000)*; Sime, S, *A Practical Approach to Civil Procedure*; and O'Hare, J et al, *Civil Litigation*.

of the dispute. These systems promote 'front loading' or the investment of resources near the beginning of a dispute to try to get it resolved quickly – even before litigation begins. For example, pre-action protocols require the parties to exchange information and discuss possible settlements before starting legal action. After litigation starts, settlement is also explicitly encouraged. The court is even empowered to stay proceedings for a limited period of time to enable the parties to attempt settlement through alternative dispute resolution (ADR), usually mediation. In these and other respects, the CPR are hastening change in the culture of civil litigation.

THE CIVIL LITIGATION PROCESS

To what degree the culture is permanently changed is a matter for time to tell. The fact remains that, when disputes exist between parties, they usually are taken more seriously when legal action is threatened or is actually taken. Many disputes that are successfully settled would not have come to the point of negotiation or mediation without the threat of legal action, or if legal action has already begun, without the threat of further litigation. But, what exactly is a legal action and what is the civil litigation process? What role does the interim application play in it?

For legal action to be taken and remedies sought on behalf of a client, there must be conduct that not only the client, but also the law, says is wrong. The existence of a legal wrong is the *sine qua non* of the civil action. If no legal wrong can be alleged – that is, if no breach of a right or duty is alleged to have been committed – the civil action will not succeed and may even be thrown out on an interim application. On the other hand, if a person alleges a legal wrong and this is proved by evidence in court, the person who alleges the wrong is entitled to a remedy. Three basic kinds of legal wrong exist in the civil law. They are as follows:

- breach of a contractual duty or breaking a promise made in a legal contract;
- breach of a non-contractual duty or conduct the law says is legally wrong. The behaviour can be a *tort*, such as negligence or defamation; or it can be an *equitable* or *restitutionary* wrong, such as a breach of trust or a failure by someone to acknowledge a right that is lawfully asserted;
- breach of a statute or a *statutory* wrong, such as a breach of consumer or environmental legislation that entitles individuals to bring civil actions against the wrongdoer.

Every civil action begins with an accusation of legal wrong and proceeds to some kind of resolution or outcome – judgment, dismissal of the action, settlement, or abandonment of the action. Every civil action has numerous stages and each of these outcomes can occur at almost every stage. Lawyers can also use almost every stage to build their case, moving it closer to one of the outcomes – usually judgment or settlement. The six stages of the civil action outlined below are designed to provide an overview of the civil litigation process, rather than a step by step guide to civil litigation. A real civil action played out to trial will always have many more than six stages and they will not necessarily occur in the order set out below.

The stages of the civil action

1 Investigation
2 Pre-action claims and protocols
3 Starting/defending legal action
4 Discovery
5 Interim applications
6 Trial

---

1 Investigation

Investigation involves getting the facts, and identifying legal wrongs or defences. Investigation is actually an ongoing process. It begins in the first interview with the client and continues through to trial. Many forms of investigation exist – interviewing the client and other persons, doing searches of public records, using private investigators, consulting experts and using procedural rules to obtain information and evidence. Investigation is important because lawyers need to have facts and supporting evidence to weave them into a story that calls for redress to wrongs or to dispute allegations of wrong.

2 Pre-action protocols

In England, under the Civil Procedure Rules, a variety of pre-action protocols are being formalised to encourage lawyers to present claims and defences before incurring the costs of litigation. According to these protocols, exchanges of information should take place before legal action is commenced. The purpose is to enable parties to negotiate and enter into settlements where both sides are fully informed.

A common pre-action protocol that has been in use for a long time is the writing of a demand letter or letter before action. Before lawyers start legal action on behalf of a client, they ordinarily write a demand letter to the proposed defendant. This letter outlines the basic facts of a claim and threatens to start legal action unless the demand for money or other legal remedy is met within a certain time.

3 Starting or defending the legal action

If a lawyer brings action on behalf of a client, one of the first steps is to describe or deny the legal wrong in pleadings. A pleading is a formal statement of fact accusing someone of a legal wrong or denying responsibility for it. In Metroland, the claimant's pleadings, or statement of claim, is a story outlining the facts that amount to a legal wrong. In the defence pleadings, the defendant denies the facts as described occurred, alleging different facts or that the facts alleged do not amount to a legal wrong or that someone else is responsible. Pleadings are powerful documents. Once filed in court and served on the other side, they are formal, public accusations and denials.

The civil action has its own relentless momentum and lawyers have to be timely in responding. If a civil action is not defended, a default judgment can be taken out against the defendant, and the claimant can eventually attach the defendant's assets. If assets are insufficient to satisfy the judgment, the defendant can be rendered insolvent. Even if the defendant has a weak case, filing a defence can sometimes provide some time and negotiating leverage. On the other hand, if the claimant starts action and does not proceed vigorously due to a weak case, insufficient resources or lack of motivation, the defendant can use the rules of court to put pressure on the claimant to proceed or abandon the action.

The pleadings not only reveal legal wrongs or the absence thereof, they also tell a story. As such, they give an opportunity to each side to begin the process of persuading the court.

4 Discovery

In Metroland, after the pleadings are closed, the investigation process moves into discovery. At this stage, the parties seek to obtain information from each other according to rules laid down for that purpose. Each party must outline in a list all documents that support or weaken their case. Then, each has a right to inspect and copy the other party's documents unless, for some legal reason, the other party objects. If one party has good reason to believe that the list of documents is incomplete or that the other party has, or has had, relevant documents under their control, the first party can make an interim application to court seeking further or specific discovery. It is extremely worthwhile for a lawyer to invest time in reviewing the opposition's documents and to identify the strengths and weaknesses of their case.

5 Interim applications

Woolf-style reforms place a premium on early activity in a legal action called *front loading*, that is, devoting time and resources early to exchange information, accumulate leverage or score a victory. Front loading can be a successful tool in preventing a case from dragging on. Although interim applications can be made during most stages of the civil litigation process, initiating a relevant interim application early in the proceedings can be an effective way to front load a case. As such, interim applications can be powerful tools in civil litigation. There are several categories of interim application. Two of them, *dispositive* and *interim relief* applications, can have an enormous influence on the outcome of litigation. These two types are the subjects of the case studies in Chapters 5, 6 and 7 and are discussed briefly below.

Dispositive applications (Chapters 5 and 6)

This type of application can dispose of the conflict, producing a final outcome to the litigation. The most common form of dispositive application is the summary judgment application. In this application, the claimant can argue that its case is so strong and the defendant's case so weak that it is entitled to judgment at this stage, avoiding the need for a trial. The summary judgment application is probably the most effective solution to the problem of defendants trying to delay payment of a debt. Delay of payment can be expensive and troublesome for a creditor client, especially if the client is forced to litigate. Summary judgment enables the client to get to court quickly. The claimant can apply to court with supporting affidavits to argue the case soon after starting legal action. By front loading, or putting a lot of resources into the summary judgment application, the claimant's lawyer can apply pressure at the start in the hope of avoiding a long, dragged-out war later.

Another type of dispositive application initiated at the beginning of a legal action is the application to set aside a default judgment. If a defendant has a default judgment entered against it for failure to respond to a legal action on time, the defendant can file this application, asking the court for permission to allow it to defend.

The defendant can also front load by investing a lot of resources in a vigorous defence of a summary judgment application. If successful in its defence, the defendant can succeed in wearing down the claimant, making the claimant think twice about proceeding aggressively to trial.

Interim relief applications (Chapter 7)

In the interim relief application, a lawyer asks the court to grant an order giving the client an interim remedy that operates until the trial or other disposition of the litigation. The most common example is the *interim injunction*, an order that stops the defendant from doing something until trial. The interim injunction application is often used as a powerful, front loaded tactic. For example, if one company sues another for trade mark infringement, it can apply to court for an interim injunction, stopping the other company from further infringement. This swift sharp move can be much more devastating than carrying on desultory litigation for many months or years.

A particularly potent form of an interim injunction application is the *freezing* or *Mareva injunction*. The claimant usually applies for this *ex parte*, or in the absence of the defendant ('without notice', to use the terminology of the English CPR 1998). It is designed to freeze a defendant's assets to prevent him from disposing of them and escaping judgment. If successful, the freezing injunction can break the other side's will to fight to such an extent that they cave in and settle. If the injunction is unsuccessful in freezing the defendant's assets, this means the defendant can dispose of or transfer the assets elsewhere. The claimant can be left with little to fight about.

Another common form of interim relief application can be found in matrimonial cases and it, too, can have a powerful influence on the final outcome of the dispute. An interim order for custody or maintenance often has a blueprinting effect, that is, the terms of the interim order tend to fix the status quo of the parties' rights and obligations. Trial judges are reluctant to interfere with the terms of these orders in the absence of exceptional reasons. So, the terms of the interim order tend to remain the same as the terms of the final order. Apart from the attitude of trial judges, another reason that the terms of interim orders for custody and maintenance tend not to change is that the parties have exhausted their resources in the interim relief fight, paying legal fees and costs. There is little or nothing left to fight with.

Interim payment applications are another form of this application, the most common application being one involving a claimant who has suffered physical injury. In this application, the claimant applies to court to ask for partial payment of damages pending trial. The court will order a payment if the claimant has a very strong case on liability and the defendant is someone who can afford to pay (usually because the defendant is insured). The purpose of the rules allowing the application for interim payment is to mitigate the financial, emotional and physical hardship that can be caused to an injured claimant as a result of the inevitable delays in the court system. To compel defendants to pay a sum of money in advance of judgment can produce the effect of preventing them from using an 'exhaust-the-claimant' strategy in the litigation. It can provide funds to the claimant to continue the litigation, redressing the resource imbalance between litigants.

6 Trial

The final stage of the civil action is the trial. The trial needs to be prepared with a goal, an effective strategy and meticulous presentation of evidence supporting the goal. Many argue that pre-trial preparation is the most important part of effective trial advocacy. The lawyers who make it look effortless at trial are those who have worked tirelessly to plan their attack or defence to achieve maximum control over the outcome. Maximum control means ensuring trial events unfold in such a way as to convince the court your theory of the case is the most persuasive one.

PREPARATION OF INTERIM APPLICATIONS

Although the uses and purposes of interim applications are similar in every jurisdiction, the procedures for bringing them differ slightly. Applications are usually heard in two kinds of venue, public and private. Private venues are often referred to as 'chambers', and public venues often refer to open court. When applications are heard privately, only the lawyers arguing the case and their clients can be present. But public applications are heard in the same room with several, sometimes many, lawyers waiting around to be heard. Local rules and practices in this respect are different, so it is essential to consult the relevant rules that apply to your jurisdiction.

In many jurisdictions, court resources are limited and both judges and masters have complained about the interim application process. Some judges are compelled to hear scores of applications in one day. They find many of the applications poorly prepared or difficult to understand. Courts have tried to streamline the process. For example, in contested applications, most judges and masters like to receive written chronologies which set out a brief history of the main events of the case in chronological order. Most courts also require lawyers to put strict time limits on their submissions. For longer applications, oral arguments must be supported by *written skeletons* or outlines. In certain cases, lawyers are even required to submit full written arguments. Some jurisdictions are also experimenting with the presentation of interim applications on the internet. In some jurisdictions, when judges and masters hear an interim application, they are authorised to award costs in a quantified amount payable according to strict timetables.

The preparation of an interim application involves two basic features – the documents used and the procedures necessary to get into court.

Documents

The two main documents used in an interim application are the *application* and the *affidavit* or *affirmation*.

The application is simply an application to court for an order or orders. The application outlines the orders sought, the identities of the applicant and respondent, and the relevant law, rule or other ground which entitles the applicant to those orders. It also states when and where the application will be heard. In jurisdictions where applications are served before filing, and only filed in court if they are going to go ahead, a separate *notice of hearing* specifying the hearing date has to be filed and served on the respondent.

The affidavit is a sworn statement by the party, the party's lawyer or witness. It contains the evidence in support of the application. Those who choose not to provide a sworn statement under oath in an affidavit can affirm the truth of their statement in an affirmation.

For more complicated applications, several affidavits may be used. In hotly contested applications, the parties may prepare many affidavits containing allegations, counter-allegations and responses to allegations.

Affidavits and affirmations often contain *exhibits,* which are copies of documents that are evidence in the case. Examples of exhibits are invoices, letters, certificates, photographs, drawings, extracts of accounts, contracts, medical reports, traffic accident reports and legal documents found in public registers.

Procedures

Step 1: preparation

The first step is to prepare the application and affidavit, and to have the affidavit or affidavits sworn by the witnesses. The terms of the order sought must be stated clearly and concisely in the application so that the judge understands exactly what is requested.

When preparing the affidavits, it is important to examine the law or grounds upon which the application is based and draft the affidavits in such a way that the evidence meets legal requirements. Lawyers must ensure it is the witness's evidence and not the lawyer's that is being presented. It is important for lawyers to remember not to stretch or distort the evidence in order to strengthen their case. Quite apart from the ethical and criminal implications of knowingly putting forward false evidence, distorting the evidence can also result in tactical blunders.

For example, clients who sign a false or distorted affidavit may want to change or retract their evidence later on when they read the affidavits of the other side. This will necessitate filing a further affidavit that will undermine the credibility of the witness' evidence as a whole. In addition, a less than truthful affidavit may come back to haunt the witness and the lawyer who drafted it should the dispute continue to trial. At the trial, opposing counsel can make good use of the affidavit when cross-examining the witness, especially when their evidence at trial is different from their evidence in their earlier affidavit. When opposing counsel point out evidentiary discrepancies during cross-examination, witnesses have been known to respond by saying, 'But my lawyer drafted it and told me to sign it'.

Step 2: filing and service

In many jurisdictions, the application and affidavits are filed in the court registry after which filed copies are served on the other side. In some jurisdictions, however, to save the costs of filing, applications and other materials are served first and filed later. In this way, lawyers can decide first whether whole applications or parts of applications can be settled by negotiation. If settlement can be achieved, the expense of processing filed applications and going to court is saved.

If matters cannot be settled or if the orders have to be made by appearance in court, the applications are filed and hearing dates fixed.

The time for hearing of the application will depend on local rules, practices and resources. The more judges available to hear applications, the more likely it is that applications can be heard sooner rather than later. Scarcity of judicial resources does not usually affect the hearing of uncontested applications, which are usually heard on dates selected by the lawyer for the applicant.

If the application is contested, court registries use a variety of procedures for scheduling hearings. Urgent applications such as interim injunctions usually get first priority, as do shorter applications. Lawyers are required to state in advance reasons for urgency and provide accurate time estimates for all contested applications. Some lawyers try to use the time estimate process as a vehicle to gain advantage. For example, a lawyer whose client might benefit from delay might give a lengthy time estimate for his or her argument in the hope that this will ensure a later hearing. But such tactics are not the norm. To ensure their business gets done, most lawyers achieve a *modus vivendi* with each other, co-operatively negotiating dates and times consistent with their diaries for the hearing of applications.

After an application is served on the other side, if it is to be contested, the opposition will usually file and serve affidavits in response and sometimes a cross-application. If new issues are raised by this response, the applicant has to prepare affidavits in reply. Preparing affidavits may sound like a rather humdrum exercise, but it is actually an important and exciting part of civil litigation. In the interim application stage, receiving the other side's affidavits is like being struck with a volley of fire; you need to return fire with carefully aimed affidavits.

When affidavits arrive from your opponent's office, clients are immediately notified. Lawyer and client then meet to analyse the opponent's affidavits, look for weaknesses to exploit and points to which they need to respond. One point to note is that lawyers often overreact by reiterating what has previously been stated in earlier affidavits. Difficult as it may be to resist fighting back, it is more effective for lawyers not to waste resources by having witnesses repeat themselves. Repetition can annoy the court.

Affidavits should contain facts, but not arguments. If one is going to argue in court, putting arguments in affidavits is superfluous. It can also reveal the lawyer's strategy earlier than necessary and give opponents the opportunity to clarify allegations or correct errors.

Step 3: hearing and argument

On the day the application is to be heard, it will usually be listed along with others on a hearing list posted in a conspicuous place in the courthouse. In larger cities, individual applications are often scheduled at specific times, with shorter applications heard first and longer ones heard later. Occasionally, a lawyer will try various tactics to delay, or to be transferred to a different Master. A common one is to arrive early and speak to the Master's clerk, advising that the time estimate for the application has to be increased because of 'unanticipated developments'. This might eventually result in transferring the application to the bottom of the list or to another Master. Another tactic is to arrive just a few minutes late, after the clerk has called for the application to start. If both counsel are not present, the application again goes to the end of the list, with the chance that it might have to be adjourned to another day. Another tactic is for one of the lawyers to serve a new affidavit at the last minute, after the service time limit has expired and before the other lawyer has had an opportunity to respond. If the judge allows the affidavit to be used, and it contains important new allegations, it may require the other party to request an adjournment to respond to the affidavit. Although practice rules frequently change to discourage these tactics, no sooner is an old tactic discarded than a new one appears.

The format of oral argument in a contested application depends on local practices and judicial preferences. In Metroland, it is safe to assume that the court has almost always read the papers carefully in advance. In other jurisdictions, where the court's workload is heavier, it may not have done so, or it may have had just enough time to skim the papers. Lawyers need to acquaint themselves with local practices and judicial preferences so as to ensure no advantage is lost.

With oral argument, applicants speak first, respondents follow and then the applicant has a right of reply. If the court has read the papers carefully, and is disposed to grant the order, occasionally it may simply ask the respondent's counsel what objections he or she has, and then proceed to hear from the applicant if it thinks there is merit to the respondent's objections.

STRUCTURE OF ARGUMENT IN AN INTERIM APPLICATION

The advocate's first consideration in structuring the argument is to meet the judge's need to understand what the case is about. The advocate can meet this need through effective organisation of information and clear communication. Below is a six-step structural guide to assist in presenting the applicant's side of the case:

Structure of argument in an interim application

1 Introduce counsel, parties
2 State the nature of the application and the order(s) sought
3 Summarise the history/facts/main issue
4 Identify specific issues
5 Address issues with supporting principles and facts
6 Summarise and request the appropriate order(s)

---

1 Introduce counsel, parties

Even if the clerk has recorded counsel's name, it is always courteous to introduce yourself so that the judge can note your name. Different jurisdictions use different formalities for introductions. In many jurisdictions, counsel for the applicant introduces him or herself as well as other counsel appearing. In other jurisdictions, this might be considered rude, and each counsel does a self-introduction. Whatever the local practice, it is preferable to introduce yourself slowly and audibly because the judge's mind may be on other things – perhaps a prior application, or some other issue with which he or she may be preoccupied.

Before speaking, look at the judge and establish eye contact to see if the judge is ready. Once eye contact has been established, you can begin: 'My

Lady, my name is Michelle Leighton. I appear for the applicant, Metropolitan Marketing Ltd, which is also the claimant in this action.'

Clarity of communication is important in all stages of the application, but at the beginning of the application, clarity is crucial. You should inform the judge who you are acting for in a very clear manner. You can lose the judge right at the beginning if the judge does not know who you are acting for or if you announce it too quickly.

Counsel can do a number of things to ensure the judge remembers who you are acting for and whose application it is as you move the argument forward. For example, if you are acting for a client in a divorce action, some judges find it easier to follow if you refer to the applicant as 'the wife' or the 'husband', or the 'applicant wife', and 'respondent husband'. (But, do not be so informal as to refer to the parties by their first names. To suggest familiarity with any of the parties is to undermine the image of objectivity that good advocates project.)

When judges are trying to grasp the facts of a case, it is easy for them to forget who is who during a submission. Add contextual labels several times in your submission to tell the judge who your client is and how the client is related to the events under discussion, for example: 'My submission on behalf of Metropolitan Marketing, the claimant ...' or, 'When I submit that Metropolitan Marketing, the claimant, performed those services ...'

Although the court may have read the papers carefully, it may have done so some time ago. Remember to use consistent terms. Labels such as 'claimant, petitioner, defendant, applicant, respondent', should be used carefully and consistently, or they can cause confusion. Try to avoid referring to your client as petitioner one moment and applicant the next.

2   State the nature of the application and the order(s) sought

You need to tell the judge why you are there and what you want, while at the same time putting it all in context. First, tell the judge the kind of legal action you are taking so the judge has the opportunity to focus immediately on the relevant legal principles as he or she listens to the application. So, for example: 'My Lady, this is an action for breach of contract' or, 'this is an action on a dishonoured cheque'. This will make it easier for her to put the interim application and the facts that support it into clearer perspective. The clearer 'the picture you paint', the more helpful it is to the judge – and your client.

Then, move from the general to the specific, describing the nature of the litigation and the application you are bringing. For example: 'The claimant in this action, Metropolitan Marketing Ltd, has brought action against the defendant, William Barton, in relation to a $30,000 cheque issued by the defendant which was subsequently dishonoured by the Bank of West

Metroland. This is an application on behalf of the claimant pursuant to Part 24 for summary judgment in the amount of $30,000, interest and legal costs ...'

If seeking a complex order, draw the judge's attention to the actual terms of the order as set out in the application. If several orders are being requested, inform the judge which have been and which have not been resolved by agreement. When you identify resolved issues, most judges are inclined to view your application favourably. It shows you and your learned friend have negotiated away some issues. This makes you appear reasonable and easy to deal with. More important, it means less court time and less of the judge's time.

3 Summarise the history/facts/main issue

Explain the case and the reasons why you are making the application in a clear, concise and convincing way:

> My Lady, Metropolitan, the claimant, designs marketing surveys and marketing plans. It entered into a contract with the defendant, who owns and operates a group of insurance agencies, to conduct several surveys and design a marketing plan for him. One of the terms of the contract was that the defendant pay to Metropolitan a non-refundable deposit of $30,000. On the signing of the contract, Mr Barton, the defendant, wrote the claimant a cheque for $30,000 and Metropolitan started work on the contract. Seven days later the cheque was returned, because Mr Barton stopped payment on it. The claimant has made numerous attempts to recover the sum due, but the defendant has refused to pay. Negotiations between the parties for the last three months were unsuccessful and the claimant started legal action.

When the facts are complex or involve a lengthy series of events, you should outline a brief written chronology so that the judge can grasp the whole story quickly.

You should identify clearly the documents you are using for your argument. When the application is lengthy and complex, counsel should (and is sometimes required to) prepare a tabbed brief of all documents, with an index, application, chronology, affidavits, outline argument and a list of legal authorities.

Then you should identify the main issue on the application to the judge in general terms:

> The defendant's defence appears to be that the cheque was extracted by fraudulent misrepresentation. Our contention, based on the evidence, is that even on the defendant's own evidence there was no misrepresentation and that, therefore, the defence has no real prospect of success.

Here, the words 'no real prospect of success' are used because they track the language of the law relevant to an application for summary judgment. To succeed on this application in Metroland, the claimant should be able to show that the defendant's defence has 'no real prospect of success'.

4 Identify specific issues

After identifying the main issue, move onto the specific ones, but do keep the specific issues to a minimum. Following an argument with one or two issues is a lot easier than three or four. If counsel cannot avoid a multiplicity of issues, counsel can prepare the judge for how they are going to be presented:

My Lady, there are four points to consider on this application. As they cover quite distinct areas, I shall be able to address you on them in order of importance.

Or:

My Lady, as the four points necessarily overlap, I shall deal with them in chronological order.

Returning to *Metropolitan v Barton*, counsel for the applicant might identify two issues:

My Lady, the first issue to be decided is whether or not the affidavit evidence on close scrutiny supports the allegation of misrepresentation. And secondly, even if there is some evidence of misrepresentation, it became irrelevant when the defendant stopped payment on the cheque but failed to notify the claimant he was terminating the contract.

5 Address issues with supporting principles and facts

After identifying the issues, the advocate should work on convincing the judge to resolve each of them in the client's favour. Mention or summarise the governing legal principle with each issue, but do not go into a detailed discussion of it unless requested:

My Lady, the relevant legal principle has been set forth in *Derry v Peek* (1889) 14 App Cas 337. There it was held that in order for fraudulent misrepresentation to be established, it is necessary to prove that the person making the representation did not have an honest belief in what he stated. Of course, my Lady is familiar with this principle, so unless you require it, I shall not trouble your Ladyship further by expanding on it ...

After discussing the governing principle, you can then turn to the facts as set out in the affidavits: 'My Lady, is there any evidence of misrepresentation? To answer this question, let us look first at the defendant's affidavit ...'

Remember that, as in the bail application, there are no witnesses to be cross-examined. In the bail application, the prosecution's facts are accepted as basically correct: defence counsel should not make the argument that the prosecution's facts are incorrect. Defence counsel can point out internal weaknesses or inconsistencies in the prosecution's case, or ways in which the prosecution's case is consistent with the defendant's case, but defence counsel should not try to contradict the prosecution's facts.

In an interim application, you should adopt a similar approach to handling the facts and not argue that the allegations in the other side's affidavits are incorrect. A conflict in the facts is a common occurrence. That does not necessarily mean one side is to be believed while the other is not. Where there is a conflict between your affidavits and those of your opponent, you might point out the conflict, but not necessarily focus on it.[2] If you want to use facts to support your case, you should compile or analyse the facts from all the affidavits in ways that build that support, rather than stress how the evidence from one side contradicts evidence from the other. What follows are some ways of using facts to build the necessary support:

- Point out consistencies between your affidavits and your opponent's.
- Demonstrate how the information in the opponent's affidavits supports the legal principles on which you rely.
- Evaluate the strengths and weaknesses of the evidence on both sides by drawing attention to the source of the evidence. For example: if the facts you are referring to were observed directly by the witness, this is stronger than if the facts were observed by someone else reporting to the witness. The weakest form of evidence is a fact reported by the witness who fails to state the source of the evidence. For example, in an affidavit, the witness might say: 'I had understood the accident occurred at 4 pm.' Here, the witness does not state who told him when the accident occurred or how he learned about the accident.
- Highlight important allegations in your own affidavits that have not been denied in your opponent's affidavits.
- Draw the judge's attention to internal inconsistencies in the opponent's affidavits.
- Point out what has *not* been said in your opponent's affidavits. Some counsel regard this as one of the most important arguments to use in connection with affidavit evidence. An example:

    My Lady, the contract contains a clause that says the deposit is non-refundable. The defendant, Mr Barton, in his affidavit does not deny he read and understood this clause. He does not deny that his attention was specifically drawn to that clause. Mr Barton, who has been a businessman for 25 years, very much involved with contracts of insurance all those years, did not draw a line through the clause and initial it. He did not make a note on the

---

2   Unless a conflict in the evidence is helpful by discouraging the court from making an immediate order against your client. See, eg, below, pp 106–07.

front or the back of the cheque saying the cheque was for a refundable, rather than non-refundable, deposit. His signatures on the contract and on the cheque are plain for all to see.

And yet, he says that he was told that this clause would not necessarily apply to him. This is essentially his defence. Yet, he does not say why he was told this or what prompted it. He does not say that he hesitated to sign or objected to sign and then was told the clause would not apply to him in order to induce him to sign. He does not even say with precision when the alleged misrepresentation was made. Against this rather vague assertion of misrepresentation with no clear statement that the representation induced either the contract or the payment by cheque, we have Metropolitan's managing director who swears unequivocally that no such representation was made ...

6 Summarise and request the appropriate order(s)

Keep the summary brief and focused. Summarise your argument by returning to the basic legal rule that justifies the application.

In a case involving a cheque, the onus is clearly on the defendant to prove it was induced by fraudulent misrepresentation. In this case, the defendant's own evidence does not come near to satisfying that onus. The defence, therefore, has no real prospect of success.

Finally, remind the judge of the orders you are seeking: 'Accordingly, we ask for judgment for the claimant and the orders set out in the application.'

It is important to remember to be clear and concise when summarising. Judges do not want to rehear all the facts just because counsel feels insecure.

CHAPTER 5

SETTING ASIDE A DEFAULT JUDGMENT

The case study in this chapter involves an application by the defendant to set aside a default judgment. Since the claimant has already obtained default judgment, the stakes for clients on both sides are high and the pressures facing their lawyers considerable. What strategic advantages does the claimant have now that default judgment has been obtained? What are the obstacles and advantages to the defendant of applying to set aside the default judgment? To put this application in a context that enables the reader to appreciate the vigour with which it is being fought, it is useful first to discuss the strategic background against which the application is made.

STRATEGIC BACKGROUND

When a party to a civil action fails to take a procedural step it is supposed to take, the other party can take default judgment. A default judgment can be taken in a variety of situations. The most common is the defendant's failure to respond to the commencement of a civil action by not filing an acknowledgment of service or a defence in the court registry within the prescribed time limit.[1] If a claimant sues for a specific sum of money owed as a debt, for example $10,000, and the defendant fails to respond in time, the claimant can get a default judgment for $10,000 plus interest and costs.

If the claimant is suing for damages as a result of a breach of contract or tort, and the defendant fails to respond, the claimant can obtain a default judgment for unspecified damages. The damages are 'assessed' later at an assessment hearing. The claimant has to prove through evidence the amount of damages but, having taken default judgment, does not have to prove that the breach of contract or the tort actually occurred and that the defendant is liable for it.

For claimants, the default judgment is a useful tool when dealing with defendants who want to stall payment. Stalling defendants sometimes hope the legal process will be slowed down by their failure to respond, or hope the claimant's lawyers will forget about them. Sometimes they hope to delay the process sufficiently to gather funds to pay off the debt or negotiate it down to a lower figure. Some people never respond to civil actions and never pay unless they are absolutely forced to do so. Some are experienced players in the

---

1   Readers should check local court rules for prescribed time limits.

civil justice system and have learned that some lawyers acting for claimants do not use all the litigation tools available to them.

Vis à vis the claimant client, there is great advantage to lawyers in taking out a default judgment as soon as the time limit for responding has expired. It demonstrates to the client that quick action has been taken, even if no money has yet been collected. It is then for the client to decide how much money they want to invest in locating the defendant, establishing the extent of the defendant's financial resources and enforcing the judgment. Some clients may press enforcement hard, authorising their lawyer to spend money on investigating the financial background of the defendant and pursuing enforcement procedures. They may want to keep up their reputation as vigorous creditors to deter others from trying to avoid debts. Taking out default judgments quickly and efficiently is part of the process of maintaining that reputation.

According to Rule 13.3 of the Metroland Civil Procedure Rules (MCPR), defendants can apply to court to set aside default judgments. The rationale behind this rule is that default judgments are obtained as a result of a failure to follow procedural rules, not because of the merits of the case. The courts will usually exercise flexibility to restore a person's substantive rights if sufficient merit can be demonstrated.

Even so, once successfully taken, the default judgment places a number of obstacles in the path of a defendant wanting to mount a successful defence. The first obstacle is that the defendant has to pay a lawyer to bring an application to court to set aside the judgment. The second is that in making the decision whether to go ahead with the application, the defendant has to consider the added risk of losing it and owing the claimant even more money in court-ordered costs. Even if the defendant does win the application, the dispute is still not resolved and the defendant needs to face the prospect of more litigation and more expense.

A third obstacle is that defendants have the burden of proof on the application. They must show that their proposed defence has a real prospect of success. In addition, while it is not necessary for the defendant to show that the setting aside application was promptly initiated after the default, the court can take into account the extent of, and the reasons for, the defendant's delay in making its decision. The longer the delay and the weaker the defendant's excuses for the delay, the more persuasive the defendant needs to be in convincing the court to set aside the judgment on terms favourable to the defendant.

The court may decide that the defendant's case as presented in the affidavits may be strong enough to warrant setting aside the judgment, but not strong enough to permit the defendant to defend unconditionally. If the court thinks the defendant's case is borderline or there are suspicious circumstances, it is empowered to grant the defendant conditional, rather than unconditional, leave to defend. The court will then order the defendant to pay some or all of the default judgment into court, thereby depriving the defendant of the use of the money until trial or negotiated settlement.

All these obstacles highlight the strategic advantage to the claimant's lawyer of obtaining default judgment, where possible, at the first opportunity.

On the other hand, a successful setting aside application can slow down or even stop the claimant's momentum. Having defaulted the defendant, the claimant feels triumphant and knows that enforcement action is the next step. In the wake of an order setting aside the default judgment, however, the claimant's situation takes a sudden turn for the worse and the defendant's begins to look positively cheerful. With a successful setting aside application, defendants can force claimants to wait a long time for trial, thereby vastly increasing their negotiating leverage. For many defendants, bringing on a setting aside application is definitely worth the financial risk.

CASE STUDY 5: *HAROLD DALTON v OTTO WAGNER*

Introduction

Harold Dalton brought legal action against Otto Wagner for breach of contract involving the sale of a car from Wagner to Dalton. In the legal action, Dalton asked for rescission of the contract and damages. He claimed that Wagner sold him a 1960 Rolls-Royce Silver Cloud II for $55,000, but that title to the car was defective, as a result of which it was seized by a bank that had registered a judgment against it.

The judgment had been taken out against Rita Dawn Vigers, the registered owner of the car. According to Dalton, the vehicle belonged to Wagner, who had purchased it from Ms Vigers, but Wagner had not yet registered his ownership in order to avoid transfer fees charged by the Motor Vehicle Bureau. Ms Vigers' bank seized the car from outside Dalton's house and sold it at auction for $78,000. The nett proceeds from the sale went to the bank to satisfy Ms Vigers' debt. In his legal action against Wagner, Dalton asked for the return of $20,000 being part payment of the purchase price, damages to be assessed and costs. Dalton obtained default judgment on all aspects of his claim against Wagner, who failed to file an acknowledgment of service. Wagner then applied to set aside the judgment.

In his setting aside application, Wagner stated he did not purchase the car from Ms Vigers. It was not his car; he was merely selling the car for her as her agent. Wagner admitted to paying her $25,000, which he said was an advance against the proceeds of sale. Wagner is not a licensed car dealer, nor has he been in the business of car dealing. In Metroland, licensed car dealers, whether they own cars or sell them as agents on consignment are, as a matter of law, absolutely liable for title defects in the car unless there is a clearly written agreement to the contrary. This rule, however, does not apply to private sales in which one person sells a car privately on behalf of another. In that situation, only the owner of the car is liable for title defects, not the agent.

Wagner instructed his solicitors to commence an application to set aside the default judgment. Six key documents, presented at the hearing, are set forth in the case study document bundle below. (Not included, although available at the hearing, are the writ and statement of claim and copies of legal authorities. Neither party filed a skeleton argument.)

Index to documents for case study 5

YR0\4239

IN THE SUPREME COURT OF METROLAND

BETWEEN **HAROLD DALTON** **CLAIMANT**

AND **OTTO WAGNER** **DEFENDANT**

NOTICE OF APPLICATION

Take notice that we, Taylor, Winslow and Co, solicitors on behalf of the defendant intend to apply for an order pursuant to Rule 13.3 (MCPR) setting aside default judgment entered against the defendant on the 17th day of June Yr0. The ground on which the application is based is that the defendant has a real prospect of successfully defending the claim.

In support of this application, we rely on the affidavit of the defendant, Otto Wagner, sworn on the 3rd day of July, Yr0.

The time estimate for this hearing is one hour which estimate has not yet been agreed by the solicitors for the claimant.

Signed:

Taylor, Winslow & Co

3 July, Yr0

YR0\4239

IN THE SUPREME COURT OF METROLAND

BETWEEN **HAROLD DALTON** **CLAIMANT**

AND **OTTO WAGNER** **DEFENDANT**

CHRONOLOGY

March 23 Yr0 Otto Wagner issued a cheque to Ms Rita Dawn Vigers for $25,000

March 26 Yr0 Harold Dalton conducted a search at the Motor Vehicle Bureau

March 27 Yr0 Harold Dalton issued two cheques to Otto Wagner, cheque dated 27 March Yr0 in the sum of $20,000, cheque dated 14 April Yr0 in the sum of $35,000

Otto Wagner issued bill of sale to Harold Dalton

Harold Dalton registered the transfer form at the Motor Vehicle Bureau

April 12 Yr0 The Rolls-Royce, licence number NC3 698, was seized by The North Columbia Bank

Harold Dalton issued a stop payment on cheque dated 14 April for $35,000

May 27 Yr0 Writ and statement of claim issued and served on defendant, Wagner

June 17 Yr0 Judgment in default entered against the defendant

July 3 Yr0 Notice of application to set aside default judgment

July 3 Yr0 First affidavit of defendant, Otto Wagner

July 7 Yr0 First affidavit of claimant, Harold Dalton

July 10 Yr0 Second affidavit of defendant, Otto Wagner

July 13 Yr0 Second affidavit of claimant, Harold Dalton

Defendant's 1st affidavit   YR0\4239

IN THE SUPREME COURT OF METROLAND

BETWEEN   **HAROLD DALTON**   **CLAIMANT**

AND   **OTTO WAGNER**   **DEFENDANT**

AFFIDAVIT

I, Otto Wagner, businessman, of 58976 The Oaks Circle, Brentside, make oath and say as follows:

1. I am the defendant in this action and have personal knowledge of the facts stated in this affidavit unless informed by another source in which case I verily believe those facts to be true.

2. I was personally served with the Writ and Statement of Claim in this action on 27 May, Yr0. As this was on a Saturday morning, I was not able immediately to get in touch with a lawyer. On Sunday, I left Brentside by car to go on a business trip to Lasthaven and asked my wife, Wanda Chisolm, to contact a lawyer on Tuesday. (Monday 29 May was a holiday and offices were closed). However, I was informed by my wife that on Monday evening our nine year old daughter, Beatrice Wagner, was rushed to the Brentside Hospital Emergency Ward because she was bitten by a dog in the neighbourhood. As it turned out, Beatrice was not seriously injured, but my wife was worried. For the next several days, together with my daughter and the police, she was engaged in a search to locate the dog. She would not let my daughter go out to play on her own and accompanied her everywhere. As a result of this, she told me that she completely forgot about the writ and statement of claim until the following week.

3. I was still away on business when she contacted a lawyer. But this particular lawyer, she informs me, would not handle the case unless she could provide a retainer of $3500.00. Unfortunately, my wife did not have this amount of money available. By the time I returned to Brentside on 10 June, my wife had still not located a willing lawyer and I had forgotten about the time limit to file an acknowledgment of service. By the time I attended to this matter and visited a lawyer

on 20 June, the claimant had already entered default judgment against me. On discovering this, I immediately instructed my lawyer to apply to set aside the default judgment.

4. In relation to the statement of claim, I dispute the allegation that the car, a 1960 Rolls Royce Silver Cloud II, was mine or that I owned it. I was not acting on my own account and made it clear to Mr Dalton that I was acting as agent for Rita Dawn Vigers, the owner of the car. Mr Dalton knew I was not in the car business and could give no warranties, whether as to title or otherwise, in relation to the car. I never performed a lien search on the car at the Motor Vehicle Bureau. Ms Vigers was an acquaintance of my wife and lived in my neighbourhood. She told me she was in the midst of getting a divorce and needed to sell her car. She knew that, although I was not in the car business, I had a lot of contacts and so might be able to sell the car for her. I agreed to do so on her behalf. She said she needed money right away, so I agreed to advance her $25,000 against the sale proceeds. On 23 March Yr0, I gave her a cheque for $25,000 as an advance against the sale proceeds. This cheque is marked Exhibit A to this affidavit. As security for the advance, she executed as transferor a Motor Vehicle Bureau (MVB) transfer form in relation to the car, but left the name of the transferee blank. It was my intention to complete the transfer form putting in the name of the transferee once the car was sold.

5. On 13 April, I received a telephone call from Mr Dalton telling me that the car had been seized the previous day. I have tried to locate Ms Vigers several times, but her telephone has been cut off. I and my wife went to her house. Her estranged husband answered the door and said that Ms Vigers had left and he had no idea where she was. I fear she has left Sedgewick for parts unknown.

6. As a result of the facts sworn herein I believe I have a good defence and a real prospect of successfully defending this action. Accordingly, I make this affidavit in support of my application to set aside the default judgment.

Sworn before me in the City of Sedgewick

on the 3rd day of July Yr0.

LC Potter   Otto Wagner

Commissioner for taking Affidavits in Metroland

This is Exhibit A to the affidavit of Otto Wagner
sworn herein on the 3rd day of July Yr0 in the City of Sedgewick

LC Potter

Commissioner for taking Affidavits in Metroland

THE ROYAL BANK OF METROLAND
42 Stanton Way, Brentside

Date _March 19, YR0_

Pay _Rita Dawn Vigers_ or order

Metroland dollars-------_Twenty-Five Thousand_----------------------

--_$25,000_

Re: _60 Rolls-Royce NC3 698_

||302262|| 004 = 068 897029=003||

Otto Wagner

IN THE SUPREME COURT OF METROLAND

BETWEEN   **HAROLD DALTON**   **CLAIMANT**

AND   **OTTO WAGNER**   **DEFENDANT**

AFFIDAVIT

I, Harold Dalton, of #27–4708 Queensway, Sedgewick make oath and say as follows:

1. I am the claimant in this action and have personal knowledge of the facts herein unless they are stated to me by another source in which case I verily believe them to be true.

2. I am in the business of luxury automobile trading and operate my business under my own name. I buy and sell luxury and antique automobiles. I look for cars to purchase in markets with low prices and try to sell in markets with higher prices. I have been engaged in this business for many years and am well known both here and abroad among new and used car dealers, antique dealers, collectors, bailiffs, auctioneers and those in the car leasing business. I have read the affidavit of Otto Wagner sworn on the 3rd day of July, Yr0, and filed herein. I make no reply and have no comment on the first three paragraphs of that affidavit. In reply to the remainder of that affidavit I have this to say:

3. In March of this year I received a telephone call from Otto Wagner, the defendant in this action. He said he was an antique dealer, who runs his business from his house in Brentside. He said that he was referred to me by Bob Waldman, a business associate of mine. Mr Wagner, whom I had never met before, told me he had a car for sale. He asked me if I was interested in purchasing a 1960 Rolls-Royce Silver Cloud II. I asked him what condition it was in and he said it was in his driveway and that I could inspect and test drive it myself. Several days later, I went to his house. He was not there, but his wife, Wanda, showed me the car in his rear driveway. She permitted me to test drive the car and I found it to be in excellent condition. It had been completely refurbished with a new engine, tyres, suspension,

leather upholstery and accessories. I asked her the price and she said $60,000. I took some photographs of it. I asked her where her husband got the car and she said, from a friend named Rita Vigers. I said I was interested in buying the car and told Mrs Wagner that I would call Mr Wagner in a week or so. Mrs Wagner said there was no guarantee Otto would hold it for me and that it might be sold at any time. At no time during my meeting with her did Mrs Wagner say that the car did not belong to Mr Wagner or that he was acting as agent for the owner to sell it. I then left.

4. Two days later, I telephoned Mr Wagner, told him I was interested in the car and, after negotiating over the telephone, we settled on a price of $55,000. At no time did Mr Wagner say that he would have to seek Ms Vigers approval of that price. At no time did he say he was acting as her agent. We agreed that, upon sale, he would give me a completed Motor Vehicle Bureau (MVB) transfer form which was already endorsed by Rita Dawn Vigers as transferor, leaving the transferee's name blank. As a trader in automobiles, I do not ordinarily do business this way, but Mr Wagner indicated he wanted to complete the transaction in this way to avoid paying MVB (Motor Vehicle Bureau) transfer fees. These need to be paid by the purchaser to the Motor Vehicle Bureau to transfer the registration of a motor vehicle to a new owner.

5. On 26 March, I conducted a search at the Motor Vehicle Bureau and found that the car was registered in the name of Rita Dawn Vigers and that there were no liens or charges registered against it. On 27 March, Mr Wagner and I met at his house. He wanted me to give him a cheque for $55,000 payable to him, but I did not have that much cash available in my account. We negotiated further until I agreed to pay him with two cheques – one payable immediately in the amount of $20,000 and one payable in 18 days' time in the amount of $35,000. He agreed. I asked him if he had paid Ms Vigers for the car yet. He produced a completed MVB transfer form signed by Rita Dawn Vigers and said, 'Harold, they only agree to sign this thing if I pay them first'. I asked Mr Wagner if he had been given a bill of sale by Ms Vigers and he said, 'No, only this', referring to the MVB transfer form. So I said that if I was going to give him cheques made payable to him, I needed a bill of sale showing I bought the car from him. He agreed and wrote one out on a plain piece of paper and handed it to me. A copy of it is attached hereto and marked exhibit A to this affidavit.

6. I gave him the two cheques as agreed made payable to him – one dated 27 March for $20,000 and one dated 14 April for $35,000. He gave me the car keys and the transfer form signed by Rita Dawn Vigers, with the transferee's name left blank. In the memo boxes of both cheques, I wrote 'purchase of '60 Rolls-Royce lic#NC3 698'. At no time did he say he was acting as agent for Ms Vigers or anyone else.

7. On the same day, I drove the car to the Motor Vehicle Bureau, signed the transfer form as transferee and registered it at the Bureau, paying the transfer fee. But I did not perform another search. On 12 April, the car was seized in front of my house by agents of the North Columbia Bank because it had a judgment against it in excess of $82,000. I later discovered that the judgment was new and had not been registered at the time of my search, but was registered prior to the time ownership was transferred to me. I immediately stopped payment on the post dated cheque to Otto Wagner in the amount of $35,000.

8. Later, I was informed by the Manager of the Brentside branch of the North Columbia Bank, Gina Fererro, that the car was sold at auction pursuant to court order for the sum of $78,000 and all proceeds have gone to satisfy the bank's judgment. I telephoned Mr Wagner several times, sent him a copy of the seizure notice, and wrote him a letter. He never replied to the letter, but said to me on the telephone that he 'would look into it'. My lawyer wrote him a letter of demand on 27 April, but he did not reply. After I gave instructions to my lawyer to start legal action, I telephoned Mr Wagner one more time and told him that I was starting legal action. I told him I would withdraw those instructions if he would return my money. He told me that he would pay me, but that he needed more time. At no time during any of our conversations or communications, either before or after the transaction, did Mr Wagner ever say that he was only acting as Ms Vigers' agent. At all times, Mr Wagner led me to believe that the car was his to sell.

9. I believe that Mr Wagner's conduct, including setting up a defence that he was only an agent and not acting on his own account, is designed solely to delay me in recovering the money to which I am entitled. I believe he has no defence to this action.

Sworn before me in the City of Sedgewick

on the 7th day of July Yr0

David Peterson   Harold Dalton

_____

Commissioner for taking Affidavits in Metroland

This is exhibit A to the affidavit of Harold Dalton sworn
herein on the 7th day of July Yr0, in Sedgewick

David Peterson

Commissioner for taking Affidavits in Metroland

Bill of Sale

RE: purchase of 1960 Rolls Royce Silver Cloud II
Licence no. NC3 698

Received from Mr. Harold Dalton , buyer, the sum of
$55,000 in two cheques payable to me for the automobile
described above

27 March, YR0 -- $20,000
14 April , YR0 --$35,000

27 March, YR0

Otto Wagner, Seller

IN THE SUPREME COURT OF METROLAND

BETWEEN **HAROLD DALTON** **CLAIMANT**

AND **OTTO WAGNER** **DEFENDANT**

AFFIDAVIT

I, Otto Wagner, businessman, of 58976 The Oaks Circle, Brentside, make oath and say as follows:

1. I am the defendant in this action and have personal knowledge of the facts stated in this affidavit unless I have been informed by another source in which case I verily believe those facts to be true.

2. I have read the affidavit of Harold Dalton sworn herein on the 7th day of July, Yr0.

3. In answer to the whole of that affidavit, I repeat that I was merely an agent for Ms Vigers in the sale of her car and that I informed Mr Dalton clearly of that fact.

4. In answer to para 4 of Mr Dalton's affidavit, I deny that I said I wanted to avoid paying the transfer fee. The reason the transferee's name was left blank on the MVB transfer form was because the transferee would not be known until the car was purchased. I was not the purchaser; Mr Dalton was the purchaser.

5. In answer to para 6 of Mr Dalton's affidavit, when I produced the completed MVB transfer form signed by Rita Dawn Vigers, Mr Dalton asked me if I had paid her yet. I replied that I needed to pay her an advance to get the signed MVB form. I told him I was selling the car for her and that the money I paid her was an advance on the proceeds of sale. I told him I needed the cheques made payable to me because I had already advanced her money and because I would pay her the balance of what she was owed less a commission out of my own funds. At no time did I indicate that I had purchased the car from her. At all times, Mr Dalton knew I was the agent of Rita Dawn Vigers. When Mr Dalton asked me for a bill of sale as a convenience

94

to him, I had no reason to refuse. Mr Dalton dictated the terms in the bill of sale attached to his affidavit.

6. When Mr Dalton telephoned me to tell me about the seizure of the car, and asked me to return the $20,000, I told him I would be happy to pay him $20,000 as soon as I got my money back from Ms Vigers.

Sworn before me in the City of Sedgewick

on the 10th day of July Yr0

LC Potter   Otto Wagner

_____

Commissioner for taking Affidavits in Metroland

Claimant's 2nd affidavit   YR0\4239

IN THE SUPREME COURT OF METROLAND

BETWEEN   **HAROLD DALTON**   **CLAIMANT**

AND   **OTTO WAGNER**   **DEFENDANT**

AFFIDAVIT

I, Harold Dalton, of 27–4708 Queensway, Sedgewick make oath and say as follows.

1. I am the claimant in this action and have personal knowledge of the facts in this affidavit.

2. In reply to Mr Wagner's second affidavit I say the following: the statements in para 4 of that affidavit regarding our conversation and the production of the bill of sale are incorrect and I deny them. Mr Wagner did not explain that he had advanced money to Rita Dawn Vigers against sale proceeds and did not say anything about a commission. When I told Mr Wagner that I wanted a bill of sale from him because I was paying him for the car, he did not object, did not remind me the car belonged to someone else and readily wrote out the bill of sale. I did not dictate the terms.

Sworn before me in the City of Sedgewick

on the 13th day of July Yr0

David Peterson   *Harold Dalton*

Commissioner for taking Affidavits in Metroland

Lawyers' strategies

Defendant counsel's approach to the problem

- My client's instructions are to apply for an order to set aside the default judgment. He says he is in the process of re-mortgaging his house, and if the bank discovers the judgment, he won't get the mortgage. Once he gets the mortgage proceeds he will authorise me to negotiate with the claimant's lawyer and, possibly, pay him something. I was uncomfortable with this tactic, because in my first interview with him I was sceptical of his claim that he was Ms Vigers' agent and not the owner of the vehicle. There was no written agreement between him and Ms Vigers and the commission arrangement between them seemed very vague. He told me he knew Ms Vigers well enough to 'agree to agree' to the size of the commission later on. I suppose that could be consistent with him parting with $25,000 so readily. But it still seemed odd, given the apparent disregard for his own financial welfare. His wife, who spent some time in the office with him, was very angry. She accused him right then and there of being involved with Ms Vigers. He was adamant that there was no relationship between them. Ms Vigers was his wife's friend, he said. Why then did he advance her so much money, I asked him – if in fact it was an advance? She was desperate for money, he said, and in any event he had the security of the executed MVB transfer form. He knew the car was very valuable and it did not occur to him that there could be encumbrances registered against it. He admits he behaved foolishly, but swears he did not purchase the car from Ms Vigers. I cross-examined him, and although his responses were not entirely satisfactory, I reached the conclusion that he could have been Ms Vigers' agent and have told Dalton that he was.

- I need to show that his defence has a real prospect of success. My strategy is to begin by confronting the two big negatives in my case. The first is the fact that the bill of sale was issued by Wagner and the cheques were written to him. This makes him look like the owner, or principal. The second is the claimant's assertions that my client said nothing to him about being an agent. These are powerful pieces of evidence in favour of the claimant, so I want to confront them and get them out of the way.

- The rest of my plan is to point out the obvious. The obvious is that Dalton clearly knew who the legal owner of the car was. The MVB transfer form had Ms Vigers' name on it as transferor and Dalton conducted a search himself that showed that Ms Vigers was the registered owner. If I put this evidence together with the defendant's statement that he communicated his agency to the claimant, there is a good chance that the Master could see there is a real prospect of a successful defence. If the Master decides that the case must go to trial, my client should then have lots of time and room to negotiate.

Claimant counsel's approach to the problem

- Otto Wagner is well known in Brentside as a swindler. But this Master is not from the Brentside area, so it is doubtful that he knows Wagner. My client, Harold Dalton, lives in Sedgewick so he did not know about Otto Wagner either. Although Wagner does not have a criminal record, my investigator reported that he has been involved in numerous civil suits, usually as a defendant. The investigator spoke to a Brentside lawyer who had a land fraud case against him and he says Wagner perjured himself in several affidavits. His investigation also revealed that he and Rita Dawn Vigers were having an affair, but he could not find anyone who could or would swear an affidavit to that effect.

- As for my client, he is well aware that what got him into this mess was his own greed. He purchased a beautiful antique car for $55,000 that he knew could be worth nearly twice that amount. He even found a prospective buyer in Ocean City with whom he had discussed a price of $90,000. That is why he was so careless in this transaction and why he completed it so quickly. He should have paid much closer attention to the details of the transaction.

- When I make my submission, of course, I cannot provide the Master with any of this information. None of it is admissible evidence. But, I can try to persuade him that Wagner's story that he advanced $25,000 to Rita Dawn Vigers is not credible. I have to be careful to attack the story on its own, to show that the story in and of itself is implausible. To ask the court to prefer my client's evidence to Wagner's is the wrong approach. If I start to do that, the Master can say, 'there is a conflict in the evidence that only a trial can resolve'.

- But I think I'll take the argument one step further and argue that even if Wagner's story is credible, when he made the deal with Dalton, his role was ambiguous: he could have been the agent; he could have been the principal. He never clarified precisely in what capacity he was operating. In a case where there are ambiguities such as these, the rule is that it is up to the third party purchaser to elect against whom he brings his action. Dalton, I would argue, elected Wagner to be principal and had every right to do so.

Oral submissions by counsel

Defendant counsel's submission	Page ref
Defendant's counsel: Master, my name is Marlene Taylor. I appear for the defendant. My learned friend is Greta Harrington, appearing for the claimant. This is an application on behalf of the defendant to set aside a default judgment entered against him by the claimant. Master, do you wish me to review the facts?	
Master: No, that is not necessary. I have read the material.	
Defendant's counsel: Then I shall go straight to my argument. Master, the rules in relation to setting aside are quite straightforward. I need to demonstrate that the defendant has a real prospect of successfully defending the claim. In deciding whether to set aside the judgment, Master, you may also have regard to whether this application was brought on promptly. My learned friend and I have discussed this matter and it is clear from the chronology that the application was brought on very quickly, so she has kindly agreed that we need not burden you with any argument relating to the promptness of the application.	
Master: I take it then, Ms Harrington, that you will not be resisting this application on the ground that the defendant was slow in bringing it.	
Claimant's counsel: That is correct.	
Defendant's counsel: Master, the defence is simple: we say the defendant was acting solely as an agent in this transaction on behalf of Rita Dawn Vigers and that he communicated this to the claimant. If this turns out to be the case, as a matter of law, the defendant is an agent and liability would fall on his principal, Ms Vigers – not on him.	
Of course, my learned friend says the opposite. She says the defendant was not an agent and that he did not communicate he was an agent. Therefore, she says, the defendant is liable and can be sued.	
To demonstrate this, my learned friend will undoubtedly bring up two points: the first point is the existence of the bill of sale and the cheques. The bill of sale was signed by the defendant,	93

Otto Wagner, and there is no mention of Ms Vigers on it. The cheques were made payable to the defendant, Otto Wagner.

The second point is the claimant's evidence that the defendant did not tell him he was acting as an agent. | 91, 92

As to the first point – the bill of sale. Master, if I could ask you to look at it for a moment – it is at claimant's first affidavit, last page. Have you found it, Master? | 93

Master: Yes, thank you.

Defendant's counsel: No one can deny the legal significance of the bill of sale. It has the defendant's signature on it and, as you can see, it mentions the car. But it is, after all, a very rudimentary document – completely handwritten and more like a receipt than a bill of sale. It is true it does not mention Ms Vigers, but then, even if she was the principal, it needn't mention her name. The cheques went directly to the defendant and the claimant says he asked for the bill of sale for that reason.

If I can ask you to turn to the claimant's first affidavit, para 5. If I can bring you to the third line from the end of that paragraph. And if I may read directly from the affidavit: 'So I said that if I was going to give him cheques made payable to him, I needed a bill of sale showing I bought the car from him.' In my submission, there is no inconsistency between the existence of an agency and the fact that the purchaser, Harold Dalton, the claimant in this action, made a direct payment for the car to the agent, Otto Wagner. Agents take direct payment all the time. They then pass the money on to their principals. There is nothing unusual about that. | 91 ... 91

Furthermore, in my respectful submission, the bill of sale does not prove very much. The defendant simply complied with the claimant's request to issue it. The defendant says further – under oath – that the contents of the bill were dictated by the claimant. Although the claimant, Harold Dalton, denies this, he does admit he asked for a bill of sale showing the car was purchased from the defendant. The defendant, Otto Wagner, gave him what he wanted as a matter of convenience. Otto Wagner was not making a positive statement that this was *his* car being sold for *his* benefit. | 95 96 91

The second point that my learned friend will argue is that the defendant did not say outright he was an agent. My submission in relation to that point is simply that there is a dispute on the facts. The claimant says there was no communication that the defendant was an agent and the defendant says there was. When there is a dispute on the facts as clear cut as this one, there should be a trial to determine what actually occurred and what was actually said.

92
94

Master, having addressed those two points, I would like to elaborate on one further aspect of the case because it shows that the defence of agency not only has a real prospect of success, but that it may actually be a very strong defence indeed. The feature I am referring to is the claimant's knowledge of who the owner of the car really was.

There can be no doubt whatsoever that the claimant knew the owner of the car was Rita Dawn Vigers. If I can ask you to turn again to the claimant's first affidavit, para 4: in that paragraph, the defendant, Otto Wagner, told the claimant he would give him the Motor Vehicle Bureau transfer form with Ms Vigers' name endorsed on it as transferor. Certainly, at that point the claimant had to have known that Ms Vigers was the owner of the car. He would know that the car was being transferred not from the defendant to him, but from Ms Vigers to him.

91

But this was not the only source of his knowledge. He was an experienced trader in motor vehicles and knew it was important to find out for himself who the owner was. Paragraph 5 of the same affidavit, Master, first line: on 26 March, he 'conducted a search at the Motor Vehicle Bureau and found that the car was registered in the name of Rita Dawn Vigers and that there were no liens registered against it'. On his own initiative, he satisfied himself who the owner was.

91

Master: We all know that, Ms Taylor. The claimant knew that Ms Vigers was the registered owner – the legal owner, if you will. The issue is whether or not the defendant was the *de facto*, or equitable, owner – and whether he communicated this to the claimant. If he did, he was the principal, not the agent.

Defendant's counsel: I agree entirely, Master, but I wanted to take the liberty of stressing that the claimant knew clearly who the legal owner was, yet took no steps firmly to establish that the defendant was, as the claimant now asserts, the equitable owner. For example, although the claimant wanted a bill of sale from the defendant, there is no statement in the claimant's affidavit that he thought the defendant was the owner of the car, that he thought the defendant was responsible for any of the title risks or that he was holding the defendant to any warranties. As an experienced car trader, he could easily have asked for warranties to be documented. But he did not do this – all of which lead naturally to the inference that he knew the defendant would not agree to document these things. He knew this because he knew the defendant was not the owner.

Master: Ms Taylor, why should I draw that inference? Why can't I infer the claimant was just careless in his handling of the transaction?

Defendant's counsel: Master, you could indeed draw the inference that he was just careless. But would it be consistent with the claimant's experience as a car trader? I submit, it would not be. For a man of experience, to buy such an expensive vehicle with so little documentation seems, well, unusual. After all, he did take the time to conduct the motor vehicle search himself. So why was he so lax about documentation? If he really thought the defendant was asserting ownership, why didn't he ask for Ms Vigers' telephone number so he could double-check that ownership had passed to the defendant. Other than carelessness, the only other explanation that comes to mind is that he did no further checking because he really believed the defendant was only an agent.

Master: Your argument is interesting, but I must confess a little convoluted. Honestly counsel, carelessness on the part of the claimant is the easiest inference for me to draw. It is perfectly consistent with his belief that the car was the defendant's to sell. Maybe the claimant was in a hurry and that explains his carelessness. I note the car sold later in a distress auction for $78,000. Perhaps under more favourable selling arrangements, the price could have been higher. Maybe the claimant was in a hurry to buy it for $55,000 and got careless. The prospect of making large profits can do that to a person.

Defendant's counsel: Master, I hear what you are saying. May I add, then, that carelessness in dealing is equally consistent with the claimant's belief that the defendant was only an agent.

Master: Perhaps.

Defendant's counsel: I'll leave that point, Master, and go on to my final one. It is true that there has been a total failure of

91

consideration and the claimant has received nothing from this transaction. My client is in genuine sympathy with the claimant. Although the claimant's loss is undoubtedly greater than the defendant's, they have both been victims of Ms Vigers' deceit. The claimant is out of pocket $20,000; the defendant is out of pocket $5,000. Certainly, there is nothing in the affidavits to suggest that the defendant was in any better position to protect himself from loss than the claimant. Both of them were careless in not conducting a search at the Motor Vehicle Bureau just prior to the exchange of funds.

In cases such as this, where the parties cannot come to a negotiated agreement to share the loss, the court must decide who bears the loss. The $20,000 paid by the claimant to the defendant was already advanced to Rita Dawn Vigers by the defendant when he gave her a cheque for $25,000. That money is no longer my client's to return to the claimant. Unfortunately, it is in the hands of Ms Vigers.

While the claimant is entitled to rescission of the sales contract and return of his money, that remedy should not be exercised against the defendant. It must be exercised against Rita Dawn Vigers. There is a strong argument that the defendant was only her agent and that, therefore, the claimant's remedy is against her. There is at least a real prospect that the defendant can succeed in convincing the court that he was her agent and that he clearly communicated this fact to the claimant.

I therefore respectfully request that the defendant's application to set aside the judgment be granted and that the defendant be granted unconditional leave to defend.

Unless I can assist you further, Master, that is my submission.

Claimant counsel's submission

Claimant's counsel: Master, on an application of this kind, the defendant, it is true, must demonstrate he has a real prospect of success. The purpose of this rule is similar to that in a summary judgment application. Defendants should not be using tenuous defences to delay payment of claimants' just debts. That is what defendants used to do in this country with greater frequency than they do now. But now, it is not as easy as it used to be. We have moved from a system in which defendants had merely to show that there was a 'triable issue' to one where the standard is a real – that is to say, realistic – prospect of success. Unless that standard is reached, neither the court system nor the litigants should be burdened with the dispute.

In this case, Master, the defendant's prospect of success can be determined from the affidavits. Admittedly, there are some conflicts in the affidavit evidence. And, it is also the case that, if there are conflicts in the affidavit evidence that can only be resolved in a trial, then the court should allow the civil process to continue to trial. But the court is also entitled to look at the credibility of the affidavits to assess the defendant's prospects. Master, to put it plainly, when one reads some of the allegations central to the defendant's defence of agency ...

Master: Ms Harrington, I hope you are not going to ask me to find that one party's affidavit is to be believed in preference to the other's.

Claimant's counsel: I won't be asking you to do that, Master. Nevertheless, I will be directing your attention to certain aspects of the affidavits – especially the defendant's – and then ask you to decide where the defendant's story as a whole should be located on the scale of credibility: is the story incredible, very credible or somewhere in the middle? How you decide this question should determine the nature of the order you make.

The defendant's story, of course, is that the car belonged to Rita Dawn Vigers and that he was merely her agent. Examined on its own, this story has several problems with it.

The first major problem, as my learned friend has already helpfully pointed out, is that the bill of sale suggests the defendant was the owner and that Ms Vigers played no part in the sale.

93

The second major problem is the nature and character of the defendant's transaction with Ms Vigers. There are several very mysterious aspects to it. For example, why did the defendant advance Ms Vigers $25,000? – not a small amount by any means.

88–89

Master, may I refer you to para 4 of the defendant's first affidavit: there he gives a reason. He says: 'she needed money right away.'

88

If someone with whom a person has no obvious special relationship, hears that this person 'needs money right away', it hardly seems likely that he would immediately write a cheque for $25,000 – even on the strength of an executed MVB transfer form. The defendant did not even provide evidence of what the terms of the advance were. Was there to be interest? When would it be paid back if the car could not be sold? The defendant also says he was selling the car for her as her agent, but there is no evidence of a specific agency agreement, no evidence she ever approved the sale price, no evidence that he even attempted to contact her to obtain approval of the sale. Although he says there was a commission agreement, there is no evidence that they agreed on how much commission would be paid.

I should point out something particularly significant: there was no evidence of an agreement to pay commission until the defendant noted this in his *second* affidavit. It is not even mentioned in his first affidavit. Another mystery is why Ms Vigers chose the defendant to sell her vehicle instead of a person or a company in the business of selling antique vehicles such as this. This, too, remains unanswered.

94
87–88

In my respectful submission, the most credible way of looking at this evidence is to infer that the so called loan and the agency were contrived by the defendant afterwards – after he was sued. In reality, the defendant purchased the car from Ms Vigers, which is why, according to the claimant, the defendant said nothing to him about either the $25,000 advance or the agency. From the defendant's viewpoint, there was no need to say anything about any agency. He owned the car. He possessed the transfer document executed by Ms Vigers. All he had to do to convert that equitable ownership into a legal one was to go to the Motor Vehicle Bureau and register his ownership.

Master: Are you asking me to infer that the defendant fabricated the loan and the agency? Are you asking me to make a finding of fact to that effect?

Claimant's counsel: Master, I am certainly not asking you to go that far. But what I do submit is that the defendant's version of events is very near the 'incredible' end of the credibility scale. Even without regard to the claimant's evidence, it is highly suspicious.

And, Master, even if you are not in agreement with that characterisation, the existence of the bill of sale issued by the defendant together with all the other circumstances makes the defendant's role in this transaction – at the very least – ambiguous. He can be either the agent or the principal.

When there is ambiguity of this kind, for the purpose of selecting a defendant, the third party purchaser can elect to consider him *either* the agent *or* the principal. Master, there are many cases that enunciate this principle and I have included two in the bundle. Unless you wish me to elaborate these ...

Master: That won't be necessary.

Claimant's counsel: Master, the claimant has clearly elected to consider the defendant as the principal, is entitled to do so and has acted accordingly.

Master, as principal, the defendant is accountable to the claimant for all title defects. I respectfully request therefore that the application be dismissed with costs.

Unless I can be of further assistance, those are my submissions.

Defendant counsel's reply

Master: Ms Taylor?

Defendant's counsel: If I may very briefly clarify something. My learned friend has argued that, where there is ambiguity about the role the defendant played in the transaction, the third party purchaser has the right to sue whom he pleases – agent or principal. I agree with the way my learned friend has explained this rule. This is indeed the rule and it is a useful one. People who are selling expensive items such as motor vehicles cannot go around being ambiguous about their role and expect not to be sued when things go wrong.

But, out of an abundance of caution, I do wish to clarify one issue: there is a difference between ambiguity and conflicting evidence. As you have pointed out, Master, the parties are in conflict about what occurred and about what was said. The claimant says the defendant was the principal and the defendant says he was the agent.

That conflict in evidence, however, does not mean the defendant's role in the transaction was ambiguous. It means merely that there is a conflict in the evidence! In the defendant's version of events, Master, there is no ambiguity whatsoever. He says clearly that he communicated his agency to the claimant and that the claimant knew he was an agent. The claimant says otherwise.

Master, in my respectful submission, this conflict in evidence can only be resolved by proceeding to trial.

Unless I can be of further assistance, that is my reply.

Outcome

The Master ordered the judgment set aside, but only on certain conditions. This is an excerpt from the Master's decision:

Master: …The most significant aspect of the evidence that has been brought to my attention today is that which relates to the defendant's payment of $25,000 to Rita Dawn Vigers. The defendant says this was an advance against proceeds of sale and that he was merely Ms Vigers' agent. As counsel for the claimant pointed out, however, there was no evidence of specific terms of any agency agreement. There was no evidence of what the commission arrangement was, no evidence of an agreement between agent and principal on the sale price, and no agreement about the terms for the repayment of the $25,000 advance. Not only are specific terms of this alleged agency agreement virtually non-existent, but the existence of an agency agreement is uncorroborated by the defendant's subsequent conduct. The only evidence of agency is what the defendant says he told the claimant – evidence that is contradicted by the claimant.

Even so, there is sufficient evidence to warrant setting aside the judgment, because the defendant appears to be adamant in his affidavits that he did in fact communicate to the claimant that he was merely an agent. Although lacking in credibility, I do not see how I can come to a conclusive finding that his statements in that regard are untrue. The defendant should have his day in court.

I am going to set aside the judgment and grant the defendant leave to defend, but only on condition that he pay into court the sum of $20,000 and pay the defendant his costs of this application in the amount of $2,500. The order setting aside the judgment is stayed until the last day of next month and shall be entered only if the aforesaid conditions are met by the defendant as ordered herein on or before that date.

Commentary

The claimant's counsel followed two important rules of effective advocacy. She kept it brief and she 'led the judge'. In keeping it brief, she focused on one major point, the lack of credibility in the defendant's affidavit in relation to the alleged agency. She led the Master to this point, taking him directly to the suspicious parts of the defendant's own affidavit. As she said,

> ... may I refer you to para 4 of the defendant's first affidavit: there he gives a reason [for giving Ms Vigers $25,000]. He says: 'She needed money right away.' Master, if someone with whom a person has no obvious special relationship, hears that this person 'needs money right away', it hardly seems likely that he would immediately write a cheque for $25,000 – even on the strength of an executed MVB transfer form [pp 104–05].

Here, she uses the defendant's own words to demonstrate how unlikely his story is – without bringing into the picture what her own client said in response. By confining herself to what the defendant said, she avoids contentiousness.

Defendant's counsel had a more difficult job to convince the judge, and it was made more difficult by an oral submission that became complicated to follow. She argued that the claimant knew Rita Dawn Vigers was the legal owner of the car, and did nothing to investigate whether she had transferred equitable title to the defendant. She further argued that, since Rita Dawn Vigers remained the owner, the claimant, an experienced car trader, must have assumed the defendant was only an agent. As the Master pointed out, this argument was contentious, because the claimant's behaviour was also consistent with his own carelessness.

Defendant's counsel managed to recover from this setback. She tried with some success to use emotional rather than logical appeal by suggesting that both the claimant and the defendant had suffered at the hands of Rita Dawn Vigers. Both had lost money, she said. Therefore, wouldn't it be unfair if the defendant had to bear all the loss and the claimant none? If the defendant could not get the judgment set aside, he would have lost over $45,000 and the claimant would have lost nothing. This argument had nothing to do with relevant legal issues, but it was effective nonetheless. But its emotional appeal to fairness would have been even more effective had the defendant's affidavit been more credible.

Although claimant's counsel stressed the lack of credibility in Wagner's affidavit, she concluded her argument with a good legal point. She argued that, where the conduct of the seller in relation to whether he is principal or agent is ambiguous, the purchaser can elect to treat him as either. Wagner's conduct was ambiguous, she argued, so the claimant had elected to treat Wagner as principal in order to sue him directly.

After the claimant's counsel had finished her submission, the defendant's case appeared very grim. By this time, the Master was probably ready to dismiss the defendant's setting aside application outright. But the defendant's counsel managed to come up with an argument which, though it did not save her client from a courtroom loss, did manage to avoid dismissal of the defendant's application. She reminded the Master that there was a difference between a conflict in evidence as to whether Wagner communicated his agency role and ambiguity about the role Wagner played during the transaction. Her client's evidence was not ambiguous – he said he was an agent and had communicated this clearly to the claimant. The claimant had said he had not communicated this at all. This was not, as defendant's counsel reminded the Master, ambiguity about the role the defendant had played. It was just that the defendant's evidence conflicted with the claimant's. When there is a conflict in evidence on an important issue, the case must go to trial.

Wagner never did pay any money into court as the Master ordered. Four weeks later, after some telephone negotiations, Wagner's lawyer settled the case. Wagner paid the all-inclusive amount of $18,500 to the claimant, thus ending the court action.

CHAPTER 6

SUMMARY JUDGMENT APPLICATION

STRATEGIC BACKGROUND

One of the most important services a lawyer can perform for a client is effectively to manage the delay and expense of civil disputes by using front loading strategies.[1] A variety of methods exist for lawyers to do this. The method discussed in this book is for lawyers to bring or defend interim applications to put pressure on the other side. This sometimes leads to an efficient resolution. As we have seen in the last chapter, lawyers for claimants can speed resolution by staying on top of a case when it first gets underway, obtaining a default judgment and then successfully defending an application to set it aside.

Claimants with a strong case, who cannot get default judgment because the defendant has responded to the civil action, can still try to accelerate resolution by filing a summary judgment application. Applying for summary judgment is perhaps the most common front loading strategy. If the claimant wins, a great deal of expense and delay can be avoided. Among summary judgment applications, the most common is a claim for a specific amount of money or what is sometimes referred to as a *liquidated sum*. Some examples are repayment of a loan or guarantee, payment for goods sold and delivered, payment of an account balance, payment for a dishonoured cheque or other bill of exchange, and return of a deposit.

Lawyers can also use summary judgment to obtain declarations of trust, specific performance of agreements for the purchase or sale of real property, and judgments for liability in tort or for breach of contract. The case discussed in this chapter involves an action by a bank against a guarantor for a liquidated sum.

On a summary judgment application, claimants must show that they are entitled to judgment and that the defence has no real prospect of success. Even if the claimant is unsuccessful in getting judgment, however, the court can decide that the defendant's case may not be strong enough to permit the defendant to defend unconditionally. Thus, the court can grant the defendant conditional, rather than unconditional, leave to defend. For the claimant, the strategic advantage of a summary judgment application is similar to that of defending an application to set aside a judgment. The claimant does not have to achieve a 100% victory, that is, judgment for the claimant, to achieve

---

1   See above, Chapter 4, pp 64–65, 68.

success. Because an order for conditional leave to defend will usually involve the defendant having to pay money into court, this can result in considerable pressure being brought to bear on the defendant.

CASE STUDY 6: *THE COMMONWEALTH BANK v JONATHAN AND ROBERT BEAUMONT*

Introduction

The claimant is suing the defendants, Jonathan and Robert Beaumont, on guarantees they had signed in relation to the debts of Jonathan Beaumont's company, Stepford Novelties Ltd ('Stepford'). Jonathan Beaumont was in the importing business, importing and marketing novelties and toys through his one-man company, Stepford. Jonathan had pledged shares to the bank and had signed an unlimited personal guarantee to secure the indebtedness of Stepford to the Commonwealth Bank of Metroland (CBM) – an overdraft facility with a limit of $75,000.

Through Stepford, Jonathan Beaumont wanted to enter a deal with Magic Buttons International Ltd ('MBI') for the purchase and exclusive right to market electronic dartboards in Metroland and Europe. To go into the deal, Stepford needed a further $200,000, having already exhausted its overdraft limit of $75,000. Jonathan told Cecilia Tourney, the bank's manager, that his father, Dr Robert Beaumont, would sign a guarantee to cover a further advance from the bank. Ms Tourney said that the bank would do so only if the father signed a guarantee to secure the whole of the $275,000 advanced by the bank.

Robert Beaumont came into the bank and had a meeting with Cecilia Tourney. He declined independent legal advice recommended by Ms Tourney and signed a personal guarantee up to a limit of $275,000. Shortly thereafter, the MBI deal fell apart. After the dartboards were shipped, they turned out to be defective. Stepford sued MBI, but MBI went into winding up proceedings and Stepford could not pay back the money advanced by the bank for the purchase of the dartboards. The bank sued Stepford, which consented to judgment, and went into winding up proceedings. The bank then sued both Beaumonts on each of the guarantees. Jonathan, whose shares had been sold by the bank under the pledge, consented to judgment, and was rendered insolvent.

The bank then initiated an application for summary judgment against Robert Beaumont in relation to the guarantee he had signed. On the application, his defence was that Cecilia Tourney had not told him that $75,000 had already been advanced under the guarantee. Had he known that, he would not have signed the guarantee. This was a defence of misrepresentation or negligence on the part of the bank in not disclosing the advance. At the summary judgment hearing, five key documents were presented and are set forth below in the case study document bundle below. (Not included, although available at the hearing, are the writ and statement of claim and copies of legal authorities. Robert Beaumont's lawyer has not yet drafted or filed a defence. Neither party filed a skeleton argument.)

Index to documents for case study 6

YR0\1876

IN THE SUPREME COURT OF METROLAND

BETWEEN   **THE COMMONWEALTH BANK**   **CLAIMANT**
OF METROLAND

AND   **JONATHAN BEAUMONT**   **DEFENDANTS**
ROBERT P BEAUMONT

NOTICE OF APPLICATION

Take notice that we, Van Langdenburg and Stolar, solicitors on behalf of the claimant, intend to apply pursuant to Rule 24.2 (MCPR) for summary judgment on all heads of claim in the statement of claim herein. The grounds on which the application is based are that the claimant is entitled to judgment and the defendant has no real prospect of successfully defending the claim.

In support of this application, we rely on the affidavit of Cecilia Tourney, bank manager, of the claimant, sworn on the 13th day of July Yr0.

The time estimate for this hearing is one hour which estimate has been agreed by the solicitors for the defendant.

Signed:

Van Langdenburg and Stolar

13 July Yr0

YR0\1876

IN THE SUPREME COURT OF METROLAND

BETWEEN	**THE COMMONWEALTH BANK OF METROLAND**	**CLAIMANT**
AND	**JONATHAN BEAUMONT ROBERT P BEAUMONT**	**DEFENDANTS**

CHRONOLOGY

19 October Yr–1 Letter from CBM to Stepford regarding facility

22 October Yr–1 CBM and Stepford agree on overdraft and limit of $75,000

2 January Yr0 Letter from CBM to Jonathan Beaumont – overdraft limit reached

January Yr0 Jonathan Beaumont requests Cecilia Tourney to extend overdraft limit to $275,000

January Yr0 Jonathan Beaumont asks Robert Beaumont to sign guarantee

15 January Yr0 Reminder from CBM to Jonathan Beaumont that overdraft limit reached

17 January Yr0 Robert Beaumont and Jonathan Beaumont attend at CBM. Robert Beaumont signs guarantee

21 January Yr0 Stepford and MBI contract in effect. Letter of credit opened with CBM

22 January Yr0 Commonwealth Bank of Hong Kong (CBHK) confirms letter of credit

25 January Yr0 MBI presents documentation to CBHK. $192,000 debited from Stepford's account

April Yr0 Cecilia Tourney informed by Jonathan Beaumont that Stepford and MBI involved in litigation, MBI in winding up and Stepford unable to pay

30 June Yr0	Writ and statement of claim filed and served on both defendants
13 July Yr0	Application for summary judgment filed
13 July Yr0	Amount owed to CBM by Stepford is $219,311.67 plus $57.28 per day
13 July Yr0	First affidavit of Cecilia Tourney
26 July Yr0	Affidavit of Robert Beaumont
31 July Yr0	Second affidavit of Cecilia Tourney

IN THE SUPREME COURT OF METROLAND

**BETWEEN   THE COMMONWEALTH BANK   CLAIMANT
OF METROLAND**

**AND   JONATHAN BEAUMONT   DEFENDANTS
ROBERT P BEAUMONT**

<u>AFFIDAVIT</u>

I, Cecilia Tourney, Bank Manager, of 342 Wildeman Road, Metrocity make oath and say as follows:

1. I am manager of the West Central branch of The Commonwealth Bank of Metroland ('the Bank') and am authorised by the Bank to make this affidavit. I have personal knowledge of the facts herein set out unless informed by another source in which case I verily believe them to be true.

2. On or about the 22 day of October Yr–1, the Bank entered into an agreement with Stepford Novelties Ltd ('Stepford') to provide an overdraft facility to Stepford up to a maximum amount of $75,000. The agreement was set out in a letter from the Bank to Stepford. It was dated 19 October Yr–1 and was accepted and endorsed by Stepford on 22 October Yr–1.

3. The overdraft facility was secured by shares owned by Jonathan Beaumont, managing director of Stepford and an unlimited personal guarantee executed by him.

4. Stepford was in the toy business, importing toys and novelties.

5. In January Yr0, Jonathan Beaumont asked me to extend the limit of the overdraft facility to $275,000. Stepford's overdraft limit of $75,000 was already exhausted and Jonathan Beaumont wanted to enter into a contract with a Hong Kong company, Magic Buttons International Ltd ('MBI'), to purchase from them electric dartboards manufactured in Taiwan and China. According to Jonathan, these dartboards had become highly successful in Asia, and under the contract he would obtain the exclusive right to market and sell them in Metroland and Europe. He needed a further $200,000 to enter into the contract, purchase the franchise and order the first shipment of dartboards.

6. I told Jonathan that the Bank would not advance any more money unless he was able to obtain further security. He suggested his father, Dr Robert P Beaumont, sign a personal guarantee for Stepford's indebtedness and he asked me to prepare one for his father's signature. I told him that the Bank would only advance the further $200,000 to Stepford if Dr Beaumont executed a guarantee for the full amount advanced up to $275,000. As a client of the Bank, his father was well known to me and, in my view, would be able to provide the security Stepford required.

7. The same day, Jonathan telephoned me and said that he would bring his father into my office the next day to sign the guarantee.

8. The next day, 17 January Yr0, Dr Beaumont and Jonathan Beaumont came to my office. Dr Beaumont wanted to speak with me privately, so Jonathan Beaumont sat outside in the reception area. Dr Beaumont wanted to know some of the details of the transaction including the viability of the MBI transaction as well as my opinion of his son's competence as a businessman. I went over the MBI transaction with him, but reminded him emphatically that all the details and figures were given to me by Jonathan. If he wanted more information, I said, he should get it from Jonathan. I gave no opinion of his son's competence as a businessman, but asked Dr Beaumont if he had had the opportunity of discussing the MBI transaction and Stepford's financial details with his son. He said that he had. I brought out the guarantee, briefly explained it and advised him he should obtain independent legal advice before signing it. He said this would not be necessary. He signed the guarantee and an Acknowledgment of Advice to Seek Independent Legal Counsel. Attached to this affidavit is a copy of the guarantee (exhibit A) and a copy of an Acknowledgment of Advice To Seek Independent Legal Counsel (exhibit B) both signed by Robert Beaumont on 17 January Yr0.

9. On 21 January Yr0, Stepford entered into a contract with MBI for the purchase of the dartboards and opened a letter of credit with the Bank on the same date. The letter of credit was confirmed by the Commonwealth Bank of Hong Kong on 22 January. On 25 January, MBI presented the appropriate documents to the Commonwealth Bank of Hong Kong and an amount of $192,000 was debited from Stepford's account the same day.

10. In April Yr0, I was informed by Jonathan Beaumont that the dartboards shipped to Metrocity were all defective and that Stepford and MBI were in litigation.

11. In June Yr0, Jonathan Beaumont informed me that MBI had gone into winding up proceedings and that there was 'no way' Stepford or he would be able to repay money advanced by the Bank.

12. Formal demand was made on Stepford for the amount owing under the overdraft, which was then approximately $257,000. When Stepford did not respond, the Bank exercised its right to sell the shares that Jonathan Beaumont had pledged with the Bank as security.

13. The amount now remaining due and unpaid by Stepford to the Bank, after taking into account the sum credited on the sale of those shares was, at 13 July Yr0, $219,311.67 plus $57.28 per day.

14. The Bank has made demand on both guarantors, Jonathan Beaumont and Robert P Beaumont, for the unpaid sums, but neither has responded.

15. Based on the facts and the advice of our lawyers, neither Jonathan Beaumont nor Robert P Beaumont has a good defence to this action, nor a real prospect of successfully defending it.

Sworn before me in the City of Metrocity

on the 13th day of July Yr0

Myrna V Steinhauser   **Cecilia Journey**

Commissioner for taking Affidavits in Metroland

To: **The Commonwealth Bank of Metroland**
342 Wildeman Road
Metrocity 6309

In consideration of your having at my request agreed to make or continue making advances or otherwise giving credit or granting time (including *inter alia* the issue of guarantees by you and your acceptance of guarantees by the Principal as hereinafter defined in favour of third parties) to ....**Stepford Novelties Ltd**......... (hereinafter called 'the Principal') I, the undersigned (hereinafter called 'the Guarantor') hereby agree to pay to you on demand all sums of money which are now or shall at any time be owing to you anywhere on any account whatsoever whether from the Principal solely or from the Principal jointly with any other person or persons or from any firm in which the Principal may be a partner including the amount of notes or bills discounted or paid and other loans, credits or advances made to or for the accommodation or at the request either of the Principal solely or jointly or of any such firm as aforesaid or for any money for which the Principal may be liable as surety or in any other way whatsoever together with in all the cases aforesaid all interest, cost, commission and other charges including legal charges occasioned by or incident to this or my other security held by or offered to you for the same indebtedness or by or to the enforcement or attempted enforcement of payment or the realisation of my such security.

Provided always that the total liability ultimately enforceable against the Guarantor under this guarantee shall not exceed in aggregate the sum of ....**$275,000.00**............together with all interest commission and other charges due to and not already capitalised at the date of demand by you or tender by the guarantor and interest at the rate of 8.0 per cent per annum on the total of the sums so due by the Guarantor to you from the date of demand by you until payment.

(2) This guarantee shall not be considered as satisfied by any intermediate payment or satisfaction of the whole or any part of any sum or sums of money owing as aforesaid but shall be a continuing security and shall extend to cover any sum of sums of money which shall for the time being constitute the balance due from the Principal to you upon any such account as hereinbefore mentioned.

(3) Subject as hereinafter provided this guarantee shall be binding on the Guarantor until the expiration of one calendar month after the receipt by you of the Guarantor's notice in writing to discontinue and determine it and there- upon this guarantee shall cease with respect to all future transactions after the close of the day of such receipt.

(4) In the event of this guarantee ceasing from any cause whatsoever to be binding as a continuing security on the Guarantor, the Guarantor's

executors, administrators or legal representatives you shall be at liberty without thereby affecting your rights hereunder to open a fresh account or accounts and to continue any then existing account with the Principal and no money paid from time to time into any such account or accounts by or on behalf of the Principal and subsequently drawn out by the Principal shall on settlement of any claim in respect of this guarantee by appropriated towards or have the effect of payment of any part of the money due from the Principal at the time of this guarantee ceasing to be so binding as a continuing security or of the interest thereon unless the person or persons paying in the money shall at the time in writing direct you specially to appropriate it to that purpose.

(5) You shall be at liberty without thereby affecting your rights against the Guarantor hereunder at any time to determine enlarge or vary any credit to the Principal to take any other or further securities to vary exchange abstain from perfecting or release any other securities held or to be held by you for or on account of the moneys intended to be hereby secured or any part thereof to renew bills and promissory notes in any manner or other negotiable instruments and to compound with give time for payment grant other indulgence to accept compositions from and make any other arrangements with the Principal or any obligants on bills notes or other any claim in respect of this guarantee by appropriated towards or have the effect of payment of any part of the money due from the Principal at the time of this guarantee ceasing to be so binding as a continuing security or of the interest thereon unless the person or persons paying in the money shall at the time in writing direct you specially to appropriate it to that purpose.

(6) You shall be at liberty without thereby affecting your rights against the Guarantor hereunder at any time to determine enlarge or vary any credit to the Principal to take any other or further securities to vary exchange abstain from perfecting or release any other securities held or to be held by you for or on account of the moneys intended to be hereby secured or any part thereof to renew bills and promissory notes in any manner or other negotiable instruments and to compound with give time for payment grant other indulgence to accept compositions from and make any other arrangements with the Principal or any obligants on bills notes or other securities held or to be held by you for AND ON BEHALF OF THE Principal.

(7) This guarantee shall be in addition to and shall not be in any way prejudiced or affected by any collateral or other security now or hereafter held by you for all or any part of the money hereby guaranteed nor shall such collateral or other security or any lien to which you may be otherwise entitled or the liability of any person or persons not parties hereto for all or any part of the moneys hereby secured by in anywise prejudiced or affected

by this present guarantee. And you shall have full power at your discretion to give time for payment to or make any other arrangement with any such other person or persons without prejudice to this present guarantee or any liability hereunder. And all money received by you from the Guarantor or the Principal or any other person or persons liable to pay the same may be applied by you to any account or items of account or to any transaction to which the same may be applicable.

(8) If the Principal shall become bankrupt or go into liquidation or enter into a composition with creditors, you shall be at liberty to prove for the whole of the moneys so owing to you in priority to any right of proof on the Guarantor's part and to accept any composition, as if this guarantee had not been given and to appropriate any dividends or other payments in reduction of any obligation of the Principal in priority to any claim by the Guarantor in respect thereof, and so that this guarantee shall apply to and secure and ultimate balance which shall remain due to you.

(9) The Guarantor has not taken in respect of the liability hereby undertaken and will not take from the Principal either directly or indirectly without your written consent any promissory note bill of exchange mortgage charge or other security whether merely personal or involving a charge on any property whatsoever of the Principal. In the event of the guarantor taking such security, it shall be regarded as a security for you and shall be forthwith deposited with you.

(10) You shall so long as any money remains owing hereunder have a lien therefor on all securities now or hereafter held by you from or for the Guarantor and all moneys now or hereafter standing to the Guarantor's credit with you on any account.

(11) The guarantee shall be in addition to and not in substitution for any other guarantee for the Principal given by me to you.

(12) Any accounts settled or stated by or between you and the Principal or on his behalf may be adduced by you and shall be accepted by the Guarantor as conclusive evidence of the amount thereby appearing to be due from the Principal to you and any payment to you by or on behalf of the Principal on account of his liability whether for advances or interest or charges and any acknowledgment by acquiescence in account or otherwise by or on behalf of the Principal of such liability shall operate as an acknowledgment of the liability of the Guarantor according to the terms thereof.

(13) Any indebtedness of the Principal now or hereafter held by the Guarantor is hereby subordinated to the indebtedness of the Principal to you and such indebtedness of the Principal to the Guarantor if you so require shall be collected, enforced and received by the Guarantor as trustee for you and be paid over to you on account of the indebtedness of the Principal to you but without reducing or affecting in any manner the liability of the Guarantor under the other provisions of this guarantee.

(14) All sums of money which may not be recoverable from the Guarantor on the footing of a guarantee by reason of any legal limitation disability or incapacity on or of the Principal shall nevertheless be recoverable from the Guarantor as sole or principal debtor.

(15) You may recover against the Guarantor notwithstanding that the Principal being a limited company may have exceeded its borrowing powers or that the borrowing power may have been *ultra vires*.

(16) Where the Guarantor is a firm or otherwise consists of more than one person the liability of the Guarantor hereunder shall be deemed to be the joint and several liability of the partners in the firm or of such persons as aforesaid and you shall be at liberty to release or discharge any one of such partners or persons from the obligations of this guarantee or to accept any composition from or make any other arrangements with any one of such partners or persons without thereby prejudicing or affecting your rights and remedies against the remaining partners or persons.

(17) Where the Guarantor is a limited company the person signing this guarantee on behalf of the Company hereby warrants that by its Memorandum and Articles of Association the company is authorised to sign and be bound on the terms of this guarantee and that the person signing on behalf of the company is duly authorised so to do.

(18) This guarantee shall not be determined or affected by the death or insanity of the Guarantor or of any one or more of the persons constituting the Guarantor but the Guarantor or the survivor or survivors of such persons aforesaid or the personal representatives of the Guarantor or any of such persons who may be dead or in the case of insanity the person or persons legally entitled to represent such insane person or persons may at any time give you notice in writing to determine this guarantee and at a date not less than one calendar month after the receipt by you of such notice this guarantee shall cease with respect to all future transactions after that date.

(19) The bankruptcy or insolvency of the Principal shall not affect or determine the liability of the Guarantor under this guarantee but such liability shall continue in full force and effect until you shall have been repaid all moneys due to you from the Principal immediately before the bankruptcy or insolvency of the Principal.

(20) This guarantee shall continue notwithstanding the death of the Principal or the assumption by him of my partner or partners or any change which way from time to time take place in his firm.

(21) This guarantee shall continue to bind the Guarantor notwithstanding any amalgamation that may be effected by you with my other company or companies person or persons or notwithstanding any reconstruction by you involving the formation of and transfer of all or any of your assets to a new company or notwithstanding the sale of all or any part of your undertaking

and assets to another company whether the company or companies with which you amalgamate or the company to which you transfer all or any of your assets either on a reconstruction or sale as aforesaid shall or shall not differ in their or its objects character and constitution from you it being the intent of the Guarantor that this guarantee shall remain valid and effectual in all respects in favour of against and with reference to and that the benefit of this guarantee and all rights conferred upon you hereby may be assigned to and enforced by any such company or companies person or persons and proceeded on in the same manner to all intents and purposes as if such company or companies, person or persons had been named herein instead of you.

(22) In this Guarantee unless there is something in the subject or context inconsistent with such construction or unless it is otherwise expressly provided:

   (i) words importing the masculine gender include females;

   (ii) words in the singular include the plural, and words in the plural include the singular;

(23) This Guarantee is and will remain your property.

(24) A notice or demand by you under this guarantee may be served by post and shall be deemed to have been duly served on the second day following the day of posting if addressed to me at address given hereunder.

(25) This guarantee and all rights, obligations and liabilities arising hereunder shall be construed and determined in accordance with the laws of Metroland.

DATED AT **Metrocity** THIS **17th** DAY OF **January, Yr 0**

Signed by: in the presence of:

     RP Beaumont   **Cecilia Tourney**

....

Guarantor

This is exhibit A to the affidavit of Cecilia Tourney sworn before me on the 13th day of July Yr0 at Metrocity

Myrna V Steinhauser

....

Commissioner for taking Affidavits in Metroland

To: **The Commonwealth Bank of Metroland**
        342 Wildeman Road
        Metrocity 6309

17 January Yr0

This is to acknowledge that on the above date, prior to signing a guarantee dated 17 January Yr0 in your favour, guaranteeing certain debts of Stepford Novelties Ltd up to an amount of $275,000, I was advised by your Cecilia Tourney to obtain independent legal advice in connection with this guarantee. Of my own free will, I declined to obtain legal advice.

RP Beaumont   *Cecilia Tourney*

....

Guarantor

**This is exhibit B to the affidavit of Cecilia Tourney
sworn before me on the 13th day of July Yr0 at Metrocity**

Myrna V Steinhauser

....

Commissioner for taking Affidavits in Metroland

IN THE SUPREME COURT OF METROLAND

BETWEEN   **THE COMMONWEALTH BANK**   **CLAIMANT**
OF METROLAND

AND   **JONATHAN BEAUMONT**   **DEFENDANTS**
ROBERT P BEAUMONT

AFFIDAVIT

I, Robert P Beaumont, physician, of 1768 Far Peak Crescent, Metrocity, make oath and say as follows:

1. I am one of the defendants herein and as such have personal knowledge of the facts stated except where the same are stated to be on information and belief and in such case, I verily believe them to be true.

2. I have read the affidavit of Cecilia Tourney dated 13 July Yr0.

3. In relation to certain events they omit important facts and misstate others.

4. In early January Yr0, my son Jonathan approached me to help him in his business. He told me that his company, Stepford Novelties Ltd ('Stepford'), was going to enter into a contract with Magic Buttons International Ltd ('MBI') for the purchase of dartboards and that the Commonwealth Bank was going to lend him money to fund that purchase as well as the purchase of other toys and novelties, if I would sign a personal guarantee for up to $275,000. My understanding at this time was that approximately $200,000 would be advanced by the Bank for the MBI contract and another approximately $75,000 would be advanced for other contracts and company expenses. I agreed to go with Jonathan to see Cecilia Tourney, the bank manager.

5. On 17 January Yr0, I went to Cecilia Tourney's office at the Commonwealth Bank with my son. I asked to speak with her privately so that I could discuss my son and his prospects with her. After an exchange of pleasantries she brought out the two documents referred to as exhibits A (the guarantee) and B (the acknowledgment) in her affidavit. Our conversation ranged over a number of areas. When I asked her what she thought of Stepford's prospects, she said she had no

opinion. I asked her what she thought of the MBI contract and she said she could not comment on how successful it might be.

6. When I asked her what was the maximum amount the Bank would lend Stepford, she said '$275,000 which, of course, is your liability under the guarantee'. When I asked her when she thought she would 'advance the money', she said, 'As soon as these documents are signed and the MBI contract is finalised'. I said to her that I wanted to check with my son before any contract was entered into so I would have the opportunity of exercising my own judgment about what Stepford was doing. Ms. Tourney then pointed out that this was a good arrangement since, if I did not like the contract, I could always terminate the guarantee by notifying her in writing. Then, she explained, I would be liable only for the money already advanced to Stepford. At no time, however, did Ms Tourney tell me that $75,000 had already been advanced. From our conversation, I was led to believe that the full $275,000 had yet to be advanced. Had Ms Tourney given me the true picture, if she had told me that approximately $75,000 had already been advanced, I would never have agreed to sign the guarantee.

7. Ms Tourney did not provide me with this information. In retrospect, I feel that, from her conduct during our meeting, this information was being deliberately withheld. From the way she presented this transaction, it never occurred to me that part of the money might already have been advanced. Ms Tourney's responses to my questions seemed as brief as she could make them and she did not encourage further questioning.

8. After a time, she placed the guarantee in front of me and suggested that I could obtain independent legal advice if I wanted to before signing it. She knew me well enough to suggest that I could give Mr Villeneuve a call, knowing that Mr Villeneuve was my lawyer. Ms Tourney knew me from several previous dealings and I trusted her. That trust led me to sign the guarantee and not seek independent legal counsel.

9. I did not realise that $75,000 had already been advanced to Stepford at the time I signed the guarantee.

10. On the basis of the facts set out above, I believe that I have a good and just defence to this action and that it has a real prospect of success.

Sworn before me in the City of Metrocity
on the 26th day of July Yr0

Barry Moberly   R.P Beaumont

Commissioner for taking Affidavits in Metroland

IN THE SUPREME COURT OF METROLAND

BETWEEN   THE COMMONWEALTH BANK   CLAIMANT
OF METROLAND

AND   JONATHAN BEAUMONT   DEFENDANTS
ROBERT P BEAUMONT

AFFIDAVIT

I, Cecilia Tourney, Bank Manager, of 342 Wildeman Road, Metrocity make oath and say as follows:

1. I am manager of the West Central branch of The Commonwealth Bank ('the Bank'), and am authorised by the Bank to make this affidavit. I have personal knowledge of the facts herein set out unless informed by another source in which case I verily believe them to be true.

2. I have read the affidavit of Dr Robert P Beaumont dated the 26th day of July Yr0.

3. The impression left from that affidavit is that Dr Beaumont was relying on me for information about Stepford's financial circumstances and his son's ability as a businessman, but that I was deliberately withholding information. This is both incorrect and a distortion of what really occurred. Dr Beaumont wanted to speak to me alone about both his son and Stepford to obtain information about them. But, I made it clear to him that whatever information he required should be obtained from his son, not from me. I was emphatic about this, because whatever information I had came from Jonathan Beaumont. It followed that whatever information Dr Beaumont required would be more reliable coming directly from Jonathan Beaumont. My responses to Dr Beaumont's questions were brief for precisely the reason that I did not want Dr Beaumont to think that the Bank had any information more accurate than anything Jonathan Beaumont could provide.

4. I certainly did not withhold information regarding the $75,000 already advanced to Stepford. Dr Beaumont never asked me whether any money had already been advanced to Stepford and it never occurred to

me that he would ask because the Bank had already provided this information to Jonathan Beaumont. He was certainly well aware of it. In addition, I am sure Stepford's accounts would have reflected this. Besides, the Bank had already sent a letter and a reminder to Jonathan Beaumont on 2 January and 15 January to the effect that Stepford's overdraft had reached its limit. Attached to this affidavit as exhibits A and B are copies of the letter and reminder. In the reminder, I added a specific note that the personal guarantee anticipated to be provided by Dr Beaumont would cover the amount already advanced to Stepford.

Sworn before me in the City of Metrocity

on the 31st day of July Yr0

Myrna V Steinhauser   **Cecilia Journey**

Commissioner for taking Affidavits in Metroland

THE COMMONWEALTH BANK OF METROLAND
342 WILDEMAN ROAD
METROCITY 6309
METROLAND

From the desk of Cecilia Tourney, Manager
Tel: (373) 929 4759
Fax: (373) 929 4788

File: Ste4007/CT
2 January Yr0

Stepford Novelties Ltd
#196–2798 Pendleton Court
Metrocity 6309
Metroland

By fax and post

Attention: Mr Jonathan Beaumont, Managing Director

Dear Sirs,

This is to notify you that the overdraft on your facility dated 22 October Yr–1 has, as of this date, accrued in the amount of $75,309, including interest.

Should you wish to extend the facility, further security will be required.

Please give me a call.

Yours sincerely,

Cecilia Tourney

Cecilia Tourney, Manager

**This is exhibit A to the affidavit of Cecilia Tourney
sworn before me on the 31st day of July Yr0 at Metrocity**

Myrna V Steinhauser

....

Commissioner for taking Affidavits in Metroland

THE COMMONWEALTH BANK OF METROLAND
342 WILDEMAN ROAD
METROCITY 6309
METROLAND

From the desk of Cecilia Tourney, Manager
Tel: (373) 929 4759
Fax: (373) 929 4788

File: Ste4007/CT
15 January Yr0

Stepford Novelties Ltd
#196–2798 Pendleton Court
Metrocity 6309
Metroland

By fax and post

Attention: Mr Jonathan Beaumont, Managing Director

Dear Sirs,

This is to notify you that the overdraft on your facility dated 22 October Yr–1 has, as of this date, accrued in the amount of $75,550, including interest.

Should you wish to extend the facility, further security will be required.

As discussed with you, we will consider extending the facility by a further approximately $200,000 upon provision of adequate security.

Yours sincerely,

Cecilia Tourney

Cecilia Tourney, Manager

**This is exhibit B to the affidavit of Cecilia Tourney
sworn before me on the 31st day of July Yr0 at Metrocity**

Myrna V Steinhauser

....
Commissioner for taking Affidavits in Metroland

Lawyers' strategies

Claimant counsel's approach to the problem

The defence is quite far fetched – typical of afterthought defences to guarantees. They couldn't come up with anything else, so they came up with misrepresentation/negligence. It looks like Beaumont's lawyer is making it up as he goes along. He did not even include a draft defence with his affidavit. He informed me by letter what it would be, only after I requested it. That does not mean, however, that we've got an easy victory here. Because guarantors don't get any consideration for their signatures, the courts generally regard guarantor defences with a high degree of sympathy – especially when they have signed for a big sum, as Beaumont has done here. So Beaumont certainly has a chance on this application. All he has to show is a real prospect of success.

Nevertheless, because it is based on an act of *omission* rather than *commission*, Beaumont's allegations are not that strong. Beaumont is saying that Ms Tourney failed to mention that $75,000 had already been advanced under the overdraft facility. Ms Tourney's answer is that she clearly told him to seek all information from his son and to get independent legal advice. He should not have said 'no' because, as guarantor, it was his duty to conduct due diligence, to make his own inquiries. The fact that $75,000 had already been advanced was easily discoverable from his son. Moreover, the approach Ms Tourney took in the meeting she had with Beaumont was consistent with her duties under the law. It was not her duty to explain the transaction unless there were facts that could not be uncovered by due diligence or there were unusual features of the transaction that should have been brought to Beaumont's attention. And even if she did have a duty of explanation (which she didn't) she fulfilled it by suggesting he obtain legal advice. She did all she was required to do in the circumstances. This will be my argument.

In making that argument, I want to focus on two things. The first is that there is considerable consistency between the stories of the two sides. I want to highlight those consistencies. When there are lots of inconsistencies on a summary judgment application, the judge will prefer to resolve them by sending the dispute to trial, where the truth may emerge from witnesses tested under cross-examination. But where there is a high degree of consistency in the affidavit evidence, there is a greater obligation on the judge to make a decision about the case then and there. That's what I want him to do.

The second thing I want to do is to direct the judge's attention to what the defendant *did not say* in his affidavit – particularly to the absence of evidence about what he knew at the material time and to the vagueness of his misrepresentation allegations. Misrepresentation is a serious claim and it needs to be substantiated by plenty of specific evidence. In this case, except for

Cecilia Tourney not mentioning the $75,000, which is easily explainable, there isn't any specific evidence I can see.

We brought this application on very quickly before they had an opportunity to file a defence. They have not provided a draft defence as an exhibit to Dr Beaumont's affidavit. Although they are not required to do so, it certainly would have strengthened their case to set out the particulars of the misrepresentation and/or negligence in a draft defence.

I'm curious as to what defendant's counsel is going to come up with.

Defendant counsel's approach to the problem

Consider this scenario: you go into the bank to sign a guarantee for your son for a very large sum – $275,000. You are a long standing customer of the bank. The manager knows you well. The one thing she neglects to mention, however, is that the son is at the limit of his borrowing power. Money has already been advanced. As soon as you sign your name, you are instantly liable for $75,000!

It is easy to believe the manager was hoping against hope Beaumont wouldn't ask her whether any money had already been advanced. If he had known, he would certainly have adopted a different attitude. He might have agreed to sign for only $200,000, or he might not have signed for anything at all. To any guarantor, the $75,000 advance is an unusual feature of the transaction. So, despite Beaumont's due diligence duty, Ms Tourney had the duty to provide him with that critical information. By not disclosing it, she negligently breached her duty to him as a customer of the bank. Alternatively, she made a misrepresentation of fact. Both are defences to an action on a guarantee.

To emphasise my point, I shall take a word-by-word look at the facts in the affidavits, particularly a portion of para 6 of my client's affidavit that describes some of the conversation between Ms Tourney and my client just before execution of the guarantee. That conversation, which is not denied by Ms Tourney, casts doubt on her conduct. It makes her look as if she is misleading him. It therefore strongly supports our theory of negligence or misrepresentation. And even if the judge does not share our interpretation, I shall argue that there is a dispute about the interpretation of that conversation. Once there is a dispute about material facts, the case has to go to trial.

Dr Beaumont, who is a sophisticated client and likes to get involved in his cases, had a lengthy discussion about strategy with me and senior partner, Tom Blaise. Dr Beaumont is Tom's long time client and Tom had referred him to me. During our discussion, I suggested attaching to Dr Beaumont's affidavit a draft defence that would emphasise his reliance on Cecilia Tourney. When he entered into the guarantee, I argued, Dr Beaumont placed special reliance on her because, as a long time bank customer, they had had many prior dealings. That relationship, I argued, strengthened the duty owed to Dr Beaumont and the allegation that Ms Tourney had made a misrepresentation on which Dr Beaumont had relied.

But, Dr Beaumont did not like that idea and neither did Tom Blaise. Tom was concerned that pleading the long time relationship at this stage could backfire. It could remind the bank that, in fact, Beaumont was highly sophisticated. He had been involved in many transactions without legal advice, the details of which he had fully mastered. Cecilia Tourney was not even aware of some of them because they had taken place before she had come on the scene. If the bank started sifting through its files it would find out just how sophisticated Dr Beaumont was about financial matters. Evidence such as this would not only counter the reliance argument, but would undermine the credibility of Dr Beaumont's affidavit. Both Tom Blaise and Dr Beaumont wanted to avoid opening up the doctor's old files at this stage. They also wanted to keep their options open insofar as the content of the defence was concerned.

Dr Beaumont also seemed negative about me getting an affidavit from his son, Jonathan Beaumont. After Tom Blaise went back to his office and I began to draft Dr Beaumont's affidavit with his help, I realised that getting Jonathan's affidavit could add a lot of support to our case. I suggested to Dr Beaumont that I meet with Jonathan and discuss the case with him. Maybe he could give me an affidavit too, I said. The doctor turned anxious when I raised this with him, giving me a non-committal reply. He said he would produce Jonathan if I 'thought it was really necessary'. His tone of voice suggested that Jonathan would not be helpful. When I said that I would not pursue the interview with his son, Dr Beaumont looked visibly relieved.

The day before I went to court, I met with Tom Blaise. He wished me luck, but told me not to worry if I did not succeed. Tom Blaise had already advised the doctor when he first came into the office that the chances of success on this application were very low and to be prepared to write a large cheque to the Commonwealth Bank of Metroland. Dr Beaumont had said he understood, but he wanted at least to take a shot at it.

Oral submissions by counsel

Claimant counsel's submission	Page ref
Claimant's counsel [*introductions have already taken place. Counsel for the claimant is Ms Stolar and, for the second defendant, it is Mr Weiler*]: Master, this is an application on behalf of the plaintiff, The Commonwealth Bank of Metroland, for summary judgment on a guarantee executed by the second defendant, Dr Robert P Beaumont. Have you had an opportunity to read the papers?	
Master: I have, thank you.	
Claimant's counsel: My learned friend has informed me that the defence is misrepresentation – that the bank misled the defendant in not disclosing the fact that $75,000 had already been advanced to the principal debtor prior to the execution of the guarantee. In the alternative, the second defendant is saying that the bank was negligent in not disclosing the fact that the money had already been advanced.	
Master: Is that right, Mr Weiler?	
Defendant's counsel: That is correct, Master. It is a slightly different defence on the same facts.	
Claimant's counsel: If I may briefly summarise those facts, Master. This part of the action is on a guarantee signed by the guarantor, Dr Robert Beaumont, on 17 January this year. The guarantee covered an overdraft facility granted to a company called Stepford Novelties Ltd – a one-man show run by Dr Beaumont's son, Jonathan Beaumont. Originally, the facility had a limit of $75,000, but Stepford reached that limit by early January of this year. The bank informed Jonathan Beaumont that, if he wanted a higher limit, he needed more security.	118
Jonathan Beaumont brought his father, Dr Robert Beaumont, into the bank on 17 January to sign a guarantee of Stepford's overdrafts up to a limit of $275,000. At that point, the manager, Cecilia Tourney told Dr Beaumont that if he wanted any information about the business Stepford was in, he should speak to his son. She also advised him to obtain independent legal advice before signing the guarantee. He declined this recommendation and signed the guarantee.	118
Because of financial reverses suffered by both Stepford and Jonathan Beaumont, who signed a separate guarantee, Dr	

Beaumont became liable for a substantial amount under the guarantee he signed.

Master, the second defendant, Dr Beaumont, says that the Bank breached its duty to disclose certain facts and/or in so doing, the bank misrepresented the facts. Dr Beaumont says that the Bank failed to inform him that it had already advanced $75,000 to Stepford and that the guarantee would secure this first $75,000 as well as the subsequent $200,000 advance.

Master, our submission is that there was no duty to disclose those particular facts and, even if there was, whatever duty the bank had was fulfilled when it offered Dr Beaumont the opportunity to obtain independent legal advice – an opportunity he declined.

Allow me to go directly to the critical meeting between the parties on 17 January. Except for one item – that I'll come to in a moment, Master – there is a great deal of consistency between the Bank's evidence and the second defendant's evidence. The consistencies in their evidence clearly show that the Bank hid nothing, and indeed encouraged the second defendant to seek more information and get independent legal advice. What are those consistencies?

First, both Ms Tourney of the bank and Dr Beaumont say he was given the opportunity of seeking independent legal advice. There was no pressure, there were no inducements. There was no evidence that the guarantee needed to be signed as a matter of urgency.

Secondly, Ms Tourney' s evidence, not contradicted by Dr Beaumont, is that she made it clear to Dr Beaumont that he should obtain all financial information from his son, Jonathan Beaumont. Dr Beaumont claims to have put his trust in Ms Tourney, but she clearly said: 'Don't do that. Don't rely on me. Talk to your son. Get independent legal advice.' Dr Beaumont does not deny this.

Thirdly, Dr Beaumont certainly never asked if any money had already been advanced under this guarantee. According to his own affidavit, there is also no evidence that he asked to see any documents, nor did he ask for any specific financial information. There is no evidence that he even asked to see any correspondence authorising the increase in the overdraft facility. There is also a noticeable absence of evidence as to

118

118, 127

what questions, if any, he asked of his son. Equally, there is an absence of evidence as to what documents he asked his son to see, either *before* or *after* the meeting of 17 January. There is no evidence as to when he first discovered that $75,000 had been advanced. Master, there is also a noticeable lack of evidence as to whether he ever did check with his son in relation to anything involving the guarantee.

126–27

All this is relevant, Master, because on the evidence of both parties, it all adds up to a course of conduct on Dr Beaumont's part that one can only describe as *nonchalant*. Here he is, about to guarantee $275,000 of his son's debts and yet, according to the evidence, makes no inquiries that he should and could have made to find out the relevant facts and ascertain his legal position. His negligence in dealing with his finances cannot be the claimant's responsibility. Dr Beaumont is attempting to absolve himself of any responsibility by alleging that the plaintiff is responsible.

In what way, then, do these two people dispute the facts? Master, they dispute only one thing: Dr Beaumont says he was misled and Ms Tourney says no, she did not mislead. May I refer you, Master, to Dr Beaumont's affidavit filed in this application. It is on the first page, Master, and if I can bring you to para 7, first line. I would like to read this aloud: 'In retrospect, I feel that, from her conduct during our meeting, this information was deliberately withheld.'

127

Master, permit me to focus on Dr Beaumont's words, 'I *feel*'. He says he *feels* misled, because of Ms Tourney's conduct. But, other than the brevity of her responses, which she has explained clearly by saying she advised him to seek information from his son, he offers no specific evidence, no specific facts, and no specific conduct to show how he was misled.

Misrepresentation is a serious claim. The onus to prove it is squarely on the shoulders of the person making the allegations. That is why, when it is claimed, one must always support the allegations with specifics. But, there is nothing here in the way of specifics. Apart from Dr Beaumont's *feeling* unsubstantiated by any specific evidence, there is no real dispute on the facts.

How, then, should the law determine the outcome? Master, the second defendant, Dr Beaumont, has to show that he stands a real prospect of success at trial. I respectfully submit he cannot show it for two reasons.

The first is that, as we have seen, the facts are not in dispute. Summary judgment applications are often defeated because there are facts in dispute that can only be determined after witnesses are examined and cross-examined in open court. There is no suggestion of a factual dispute here. It would hardly be worth the court's time or the parties' money to drag out this litigation and conduct a full trial.

The second reason is the law. It is on the side of the claimant. Permit me to sum up the cases that I have provided to you in the bundle of authorities. Whether the defence is framed in negligence or misrepresentation, the principles are similar. Master, in a situation where someone goes into a bank to sign a guarantee, there exists between the bank and the guarantor a shared responsibility when it comes to ascertaining all the relevant facts.

As a general rule, Master, it is the guarantor's responsibility to determine all the relevant facts by the exercise of due diligence. If there are relevant facts the guarantor cannot find out through due diligence or if there is some unusual feature of the transaction, then responsibility to disclose facts can, depending on the circumstances, shift to the bank.

Master, I submit that in this case that responsibility does not shift to the bank. The second defendant, Dr Beaumont, could have discovered all the relevant facts by due diligence and there were no unusual features that needed to be disclosed.

This can be demonstrated first by looking at exhibits A and B of Ms Tourney's second affidavit.

First, exhibit A: on 2 January, the first defendant was notified by fax that approximately $75,000 had already been advanced, and if he wanted more money, the bank required further security. On the next page, Master, is exhibit B, faxed to the first defendant just two days before his father signed the guarantee.

130

131

As you can see Master, it clearly states again that $75,550 has been advanced and that a further $200,000 credit will be extended with adequate security. This was not hidden. The second defendant could easily have discovered it by due diligence – by doing as the bank suggested – by seeking further information from his son and the advice of a lawyer.

I have one final point, Master: the fact that money had already been advanced is not, I submit, an unusual feature of a guarantee transaction. It is very common. It is to be expected. And just about every guarantee document plainly says so.

Even if the second defendant did not understand the document – and there is no evidence of this – he was most emphatically told to make his own inquiries and to obtain legal advice on it. Ms. Tourney clearly defined Dr Beaumont's responsibilities and gave him the opportunity to carry them out. He declined this opportunity.

Master, on this last point, if I could turn your attention to *Shotter v Westpac Banking Corporation* [1988] 2 New Zealand Law Reports 316. This is a case listed in my learned friend's bundle of authorities at tab 1. It involved a situation in which the guarantor as customer of a bank signed a guarantee and was unaware of a specific liability that the guarantee covered. The bank did not inform him of this liability and the court held that the bank's negligent breach of duty in not informing him invalidated the guarantee to the extent of that specific liability. If I can bring you, Master, to p 336 of the case, fourth line from the bottom. The court had this to say:

'Where the guarantor is a customer of the bank and a situation arises where the bank should reasonably suspect that its customer may not fully understand the meaning of the guarantee and the extent of the liability undertaken thereby or that there is some special circumstance known to the bank which the bank should reasonably suspect might not be known to the guarantor then there is a duty of explanation, warning or *recommendation of separate legal advice.*'

Master, I stress those final words 'recommendation of separate legal advice' because, in the *Shotter* case, there was no recommendation of separate legal advice and no legal advice was given. Even if it could be held that the bank should have suspected that Dr Beaumont was unaware of the $75,000 advance, the Commonwealth Bank has covered itself completely in this situation. It has fulfilled its duty to the second defendant by giving him the opportunity to obtain legal advice – an opportunity he failed to take advantage of.

For these reasons, I submit that the second defendant, Dr Robert Beaumont, has failed to make out a case of either negligence or misrepresentation and has thus failed to show he has a real prospect of success. Judgment should be entered in the claimant's favour with costs.

Unless I can assist you further, Master, those are my submissions.

Defendant counsel's submission:

Master: Thank you, Ms Stolar. I'll hear from you, Mr Weiler

Defendant's counsel: Master, what I seek to demonstrate is that there is ample evidence that the second defendant has a real prospect of success in his defence.

The circumstances of this case raise two important points: the first is that the bank owed the second defendant, as a customer of the bank, a duty to disclose the fact that $75,000 had already been advanced, but that it negligently failed to do so. The second is that, contrary to what my learned friend has so eloquently submitted, there are factual issues with regard to negligence or misrepresentation that need sorting out at trial.

Master, on to the first point – that the bank owed the second defendant, as a customer of the bank, a duty to disclose the $75,000 advance.

Master, if I can trouble you to look again at the *Shotter* case at tab 1 of the bundle. If I may, I would like to refer to the same quotation as my learned friend at the bottom of p 336. I'll repeat some of it:

'... a situation arises where the bank should reasonably suspect that its customer may not fully understand the meaning of the guarantee and the extent of the liability undertaken thereby ... then there is a duty of explanation, warning or recommendation of separate legal advice.'

This is one of the points made by the court in *The Royal Bank of Canada v Oram et al* [1978] 1 Western Weekly Reports 564. At tab 5, Master: as in the case at bar, the guarantor in that case operated under the mistaken belief that he was only guaranteeing future debt, not past debt. Even though what the assistant manager did in the *Royal Bank* case was quite innocent, he induced the mistake and the guarantor was relieved of liability under the guarantee. Although this is a case characterised as mistake of fact, the issues are similar. If I can lead you, Master, to p 572, first paragraph, sixth line from the bottom of that paragraph. The court said:

'I would have to find that in the circumstances [the assistant manager] would know that at the very least Mr Oram [the guarantor] was under some misapprehension as to the actual terms of this guarantee and, in particular, the term that he was being required to guarantee the past indebtedness of the company to the bank.'

Master, there is one important fact that shows Cecilia Tourney should have suspected, or known, the second defendant did not fully understand the meaning of this guarantee, that he was in the dark and uneasy about the transaction and required more information from the bank. The second defendant asked to speak with Ms Tourney privately, wanting to know details of the transaction. Obviously, he had some concerns that Ms Tourney could have addressed. She was certainly put on notice or at least should have been alerted to the possibility that the second defendant had doubts in relation to the proposed transaction.

118

At that point, she should have known that the second defendant may have been having difficulty getting all the relevant information – that he may not have trusted his son. For what other reason would he have tried to obtain information – information that included her views on his son's competence? This surely must have alerted her to the necessity of being totally forthcoming about providing more information.

118

Another point to highlight here, Master, is that the fact that $75,000 was already advanced is not just another miscellaneous piece of information to be ascertained by asking the son, who could very well have concealed it. This is a very critical piece of information, Master. In short, it is an unusual feature of the transaction, requiring disclosure. To the bank, it means as soon as you put your signature on this guarantee, you are immediately liable for $75,000. As Ms Tourney watched the second defendant signing the guarantee, surely one of the first things that would have come to her mind was this: what a relief! Now I've got that $75,000 secured.

Of course, there is no specific evidence that this is what did occur to her. She has not yet been cross-examined. But, surely, the circumstances strongly suggest that it did occur to her or should have. If so, she had the duty to volunteer that information right away – without any hesitation. I might add here, Master, that the fact that the bank sent two letters in January reminding Jonathan Beaumont that his overdraft had reached its limit is not relevant. Those letters were not sent to my client and there is no evidence he saw them.

Master: That is all very well, Mr Weiler. But the *Shotter* case says that the failure to disclose, in effect, can be cured with the recommendation of independent legal advice. The Commonwealth Bank recommended independent legal advice in this case, so the failure to disclose is cured. Isn't it? Your learned friend is saying the bank has fulfilled its duty.

Defendant's counsel: With respect, Master, I do not believe *Shotter* decided that the recommendation of legal advice necessarily cures either negligence or misrepresentation. There was no such recommendation in *Shotter*, so we do not know what the outcome would have been had there been such a recommendation of legal advice. I do not think my learned friend would disagree with the principle that if a misrepresentation – even if innocent – induces someone to sign a guarantee, the court has jurisdiction to grant relief whether or not there has been independent legal advice.

Which brings me to my second point, Master – a point that is at the heart of my client's response to this application for summary judgment: there *was* a misrepresentation that induced him to sign. At the very least, there is a very real dispute about whether there was a misrepresentation. It all comes down to a question of fact. Did Ms Tourney misrepresent a critical fact or didn't she? If she did, then I submit that the fact that Dr Beaumont was given the opportunity to obtain legal advice is beside the point.

My learned friend says there is no specific evidence that she misled Dr Beaumont. We say there is. For there to be such evidence, Master, there need not be a specific misrepresentation in words. Misrepresentation by conduct or omission can be effective and it was effective here, operating on the mind of the second defendant, Dr Beaumont.

129–31

As it happens, Master, in this case, there was misrepresentation by omission, but there is also some evidence of an active misrepresentation, not just a passive one. Master, if you wouldn't mind looking again at the second defendant's affidavit, at para 6.

127

Please note that the second defendant, according to his evidence, asked for the maximum amount the bank would lend to Stepford. Ms Tourney replied: '$275,000.'

Master, she did not say: '$200,000, because the bank has already advanced $75,000.' She said simply: '$275,000.' Now, Master, a charitable interpretation of that statement is that it is ambiguous; the less charitable interpretation is that it is deliberately misleading. Either way, Master, it is a misrepresentation and, either way, this exchange is not denied in Ms Tourney's second affidavit.

127

Ms Tourney carried the misrepresentation even further when the second defendant then asked her 'when she thought she would advance the money'. Master, here again she had a golden opportunity to correct the misunderstanding, because the money he was referring to was obviously $275,000 and not $200,000. She did not correct the misunderstanding, but answered the question directly: 'As soon as these documents are signed and the MBI contract is finalised.'

127

127

Again, Master, this exchange is not denied in Ms Tourney's second affidavit. Any listener must conclude from this exchange that, when the documents were signed, the bank was going to advance $275,000. But, Master, we all know that was not the case. Only $200,000 was advanced. That, Master, is the essence of the misrepresentation – or the negligence. Master, with respect, I do not see how that could have been cured by a recommendation of legal advice. Even had my client taken legal advice, his mind would still be operating under mistaken facts. Legal advice might not have corrected them.

128–29

I respectfully submit that, on the basis of the evidence in the affidavits you have before you, Master, the second defendant, Dr Beaumont, not only has a real prospect of success, he has a good prospect of success. For these reasons, I respectfully submit that the claimant's application should be dismissed with costs and the second defendant should be given unconditional leave to defend.

Unless I can be of further assistance, those are my submissions.

Claimant counsel's reply

Master: Ms Stolar, you can reply if you like.

Claimant's counsel: Thank you, Master. In reply, I would like to draw your attention to one suggestion that my learned friend raised in relation to his defence. At the centre of this defence is the allegation that Ms Tourney negligently withheld information that $75,000 had already been advanced. Central to this allegation is the suggestion made by my learned friend that, because the second defendant wanted to speak to her privately, Ms Tourney should have known, or suspected, that the second defendant was having difficulty getting information from his son. And, that she should have known that the second defendant may not have trusted his son. And that, for that reason, she should have been – to use my learned friend's term – 'totally forthcoming'.

Master, that suggestion is surely speculation upon speculation. It is simply not supported in the slightest way by the facts before you. There is no evidence that the second defendant was having difficulty getting information from his son. There is no evidence that he did not trust his son to give him information. There is no evidence that he communicated any of this to Ms Tourney explicitly or even implicitly. There is no evidence about what passed between father and son in relation to the guarantee either before or after he signed it.

According to the second defendant's own evidence, the reason he wanted to speak to Ms Tourney privately was to discuss his son's 'prospects' and the 'MBI contract'. That is hardly a basis for inferring that Ms Tourney should have known anything at all about the relationship between father and son, let alone that the father was allegedly having difficulty getting information from the son. It is hardly a basis for inferring Ms Tourney concealed relevant information, the disclosure of which would have affected his decision to sign the guarantee.

The most logical inference to draw in this situation is that Ms Tourney was very careful not to mislead and not to conceal. She clearly invited the second defendant to get all relevant information from his son. Whether or not the second defendant complied is unknown. We don't know because there is no evidence about this. What we do know is that the second defendant is now holding Ms Tourney responsible for incurring a liability that I respectfully submit he and he alone should be responsible for.

Unless I can assist you further, those are my submissions.

Outcome

What follows is an excerpt from the Master's decision:

Master: ... I do not agree with counsel for the claimant when she says Dr Beaumont was nonchalant in relation to his duties as a guarantor. He was definitely concerned enough about the transaction he was entering into to make inquiries of the bank manager in relation to the MBI transaction and his son's competence. He seems, however, to have been distracted by the MBI transaction and appears not to have made a wider range of inquiries of both his son and the bank. Had he, for example, looked at his son's documents, he would have seen that Stepford's overdraft facility of $75,000 was already exhausted. I do find it somewhat odd that a man of his experience did not make sufficient inquiries to discover this. I also note the fact that he offered no evidence about what inquiries, if any, he did make of his son. He certainly offered no evidence that his son concealed any information.

He also declined independent legal advice. Had he had such advice, it is certainly more likely (but by no means certain) that the advice would have triggered an inquiry about advances already made. After all, the very first line of the guarantee reminds the reader that the guarantee is meant to secure *existing* as well as future loans. It says: 'In consideration of your having at my request agreed to make or continue making advances ... I, the undersigned (hereinafter called "the Guarantor") hereby agree to pay to you on demand all sums of money which are now or shall at any time be owing to you anywhere on any account whatsoever ...' So, it is reasonable to draw the inference that Dr Beaumont made insufficient inquiries. On the evidence before me, I am satisfied he did not meet his duty of due diligence.

On the other hand, it is not difficult to imagine how he could have overlooked the obvious. Even had he received independent legal advice, the existing advance of $75,000 might still have been overlooked. Guarantee documents such as this one are full of standard clauses, and there are some solicitors who might not have been so struck by the standard clauses in the first line that they would have immediately advised their client to inquire about existing advances. I agree with Mr Weiler, counsel for Dr Beaumont, when he argues that the prior advance of $75,000 is fundamental to the transaction, and that the bank should have volunteered it. I am not saying that, in all cases, the bank is under a duty to inform the guarantor that there are pre-existing advances. But, where the guarantor is also a customer of the bank, the existence of that duty is more likely in circumstances where there is reason to suspect that the guarantor does not fully grasp all the important details of the transaction.

Moreover, Mr Weiler argues that Dr Beaumont did not fully grasp the details because he was misled. While I am not prepared to decide at this stage if he was or was not misled, I do agree that there is at least a real dispute about the facts on that issue. If Dr Beaumont proves those facts at trial, he is very likely to have a good defence of negligence or misrepresentation. As such, the defence has a real prospect of success at this stage.

In these circumstances, I am granting the second defendant unconditional leave to defend ...

Commentary

As a guarantor, Dr Beaumont appeared very lackadaisical toward his duty of due diligence, but Mr Weiler managed to shift the blame for this financial fiasco on to Ms Tourney by carefully dissecting the Tourney/Beaumont conversation. He made the facts come alive, by focusing on the specific words used in para 6 of his client's affidavit. He used these to demonstrate that a case could be made that Ms Tourney negligently concealed the $75,000 advance. Then he reminded the court that none of this conversation contained in his client's affidavit had been denied in the claimant's affidavit. When an allegation is made in an affidavit and it is not denied, the advocate can argue it should be treated as fact. Mr Weiler did well to remind the court that Ms Tourney did not deny the conversation took place. This is a classic example of how counsel focused on the facts.

While Mr Weiler perhaps stretched the interpretation of that conversation, he made it virtually impossible for claimant's counsel to argue a different interpretation. If she were to do so, she would have fallen into his trap. Mr Weiler could then have reminded the court that their differing interpretations showed there was indeed a dispute on the facts and, when there is a factual dispute, there must be a trial.

In approaching the problem, Mr Weiler stuck to his theory, focusing on one simple point: his client should have known about the prior $75,000 advance and Ms Tourney should have told him about it before he signed the guarantee.

As for claimant's counsel, Ms Stolar, she may have committed two errors that adversely affected her case. The first is that she failed to comment on the absence of an affidavit sworn by Jonathan Beaumont. Jonathan Beaumont could have corroborated his father's story in a number of ways, particularly about when his father first knew that $75,000 had already been advanced to Stepford at the time he executed the guarantee. The absence of an affidavit from the only other crucial witness in the case weakens the credibility of Dr Beaumont's story. She should have stressed this point.

The second is that she was over-confident. Her goal may have been too ambitious. In explaining her approach to the problem, she belittled the second defendant's defence and risked all to obtain summary judgment.

What she might have done instead was to scale back her goal, aim for conditional leave to defend and an order that the defendant pay money into court. This she might have achieved by drawing more attention to the lack of credibility in Dr Beaumont's affidavit, in particular para 4 (above, p 126), a paragraph that seems to have escaped Ms Stolar's attention:

> In early January Yr0, my son Jonathan approached me to help him in his business. He told me that his company, Stepford Novelties Ltd ('Stepford') was going to enter into a contract with Magic Buttons International Ltd ('MBI') for the purchase of dartboards and that the Commonwealth Bank was going to lend him money to fund that purchase as well as the purchase of other toys and novelties, if I would sign a personal guarantee for up to $275,000. *My understanding at this time was that approximately $200,000 would be advanced by the Bank for the MBI contract and another approximately $75,000 would be advanced for other contracts and company expenses.* I agreed to go with Jonathan to see Cecilia Tourney, the bank manager.

The italicised words suggest that someone told Dr Beaumont that the full $275,000 would be advanced. But the words are both carefully contrived and very vague. Dr Beaumont does not say *who* told him 'another $75,000 would be advanced for other contracts and company expenses'. The source of his knowledge is left undisclosed and, in affidavits, sources of knowledge should be disclosed. If they are not, it can make the statement look dubious – as it does here. In addition, Dr Beaumont does not specify which 'other contracts' he is referring to. Ms Stolar could have argued that this vagueness – vagueness which is reinforced by his vague assertions of being misled – weakens the doctor's credibility.

Against this vagueness, Ms Stolar could have juxtaposed Cecilia Tourney's letter to Jonathan Beaumont dated 15 January Yr0 (above, p 131), attached as exhibit B to her second affidavit. Although Ms Stolar did mention this letter toward the end of her first submission, she did not contrast its clarity with Dr Beaumont's vagueness. This letter shows vividly that, only two days before Dr Beaumont signed the guarantee, the bank had communicated to Jonathan Beaumont in crystal clear language that any new security to be provided to the bank would clearly cover the $75,000 already advanced. Although not communicated directly to Dr Beaumont, this letter does show that the bank put all its cards on the table – in writing. Ms Tourney had no reason to expect that Jonathan Beaumont would conceal this letter from his father.

By arguing a lack of credibility and focusing on the details of the documentary evidence, Ms Stolar might have succeeded in persuading the court to order Dr Beaumont to pay money into court. This would have put her client in a much stronger position.

CHAPTER 7

APPLICATION FOR INTERIM PAYMENT

STRATEGIC BACKGROUND

Although not nearly as expensive as a trial, an interim application can be a costly procedure for both the party bringing it and the party defending it. The civil justice reforms carefully considered this issue and have explicitly incorporated cost consciousness into the new ethos. As a result, before bringing an application, lawyers need to justify the expense to the client and be prepared to justify it to the court. The case study in this chapter illustrates a lawyer's efforts in doing this. While the lawyer has no difficulty justifying the application to his client, he faces a challenge when he tries to justify it to the court. The application is one for interim payment and the amount requested is small compared to the cost of bringing it. The applicant's lawyer devises a strategy to persuade the court that his application is designed not to increase costs unnecessarily, but to promote negotiation and settlement.

In the case study, I have adopted the overriding objective of the English Civil Procedure Rules (CPR) as the overriding objective for the Metroland Civil Procedure Rules. That overriding objective (r 1.1 of the MCPR) is 'to deal with cases justly'. This means that the court should ensure that the parties are on an equal footing, the expense is kept to a minimum, and the case is dealt with in ways that are proportionate to these factors:

- amount of money involved;
- importance of the case;
- complexity of the issues; and
- financial position of each party.

The new ethos that r 1.1 exemplifies is designed to increase fairness by discouraging unnecessary procedures that increase expense or delay the resolution of disputes.

In spite of the existence of this overriding objective, civil litigation can still be a protracted, expensive and disheartening process. Cases can span years, and when they do, justice delayed really does turn out to be justice denied. Even if the claimant's case is rock solid and the claimant is certain to be awarded damages at trial, a delayed resolution can lead to great hardship. A passenger in a motor vehicle severely injured in a collision, for example, is bound to get damages at trial. But, as the litigation drags on, the daily discomfort of the claimant's life, and the inevitable financial pain caused by the injury are certain to wear the claimant down, reducing the will to litigate further. This lowers the claimant's expectations and decreases the likelihood of a fair settlement.

The interim payment application, available to litigants both before and after the reforms, is designed to prevent, or at least mitigate the effects of, unjust delays in such a situation. On an application for interim payment, if you can show that your client has a very strong case on liability and that the client will be awarded a substantial amount of money in damages, the court can order the defendant to make an interim payment. The court has the discretion to order an interim payment to the claimant in an amount which is a 'reasonable proportion' of the likely amount of the final judgment (MCPR r 25.7). In this way, the interim payment application is designed to relieve the hardship of being a claimant with little money, suing someone (for example, an insurance company) with substantial resources, who is not in a hurry to settle.

In exercising its discretion, the court will look at the financial position of each of the parties and try to redress financial inequality by giving the claimant enough money to continue pursuing the litigation, but not so much as to risk the claimant being awarded at trial less than the amount of the interim payment. From a strategic viewpoint, the successful interim payment application is an 'equaliser'. It is designed to reduce both the claimant's anxiety and the financial pressure the claimant is under, thereby increasing the claimant's capacity to carry on the litigation and apply pressure to the defendant.

Personal injury litigation is probably the most common context for the interim payment application, but it is not the only one. In case study 7, a property owner is suing for possession of his property and is applying for an interim payment of rent from the person who he says is unlawfully occupying it.

The applicable rule is r 25.7(1)(d) of the Metroland Civil Procedure Rules. Under this rule, the court may order an interim payment if (1) the claimant is seeking an order for possession of land and (2) the court is satisfied that, at trial, the defendant would be held liable to pay the claimant occupation rent while the claim for possession was pending. Whatever the anticipated outcome as to who is entitled to possession, the court can order an interim payment to the property owner if it finds that the claimant would be entitled to rent as a result of the defendant's occupation of the property.

The purpose behind the rule is similar to that governing interim payments in a case of personal injury. It is to prevent a defendant from taking advantage of an unresolved possession dispute by remaining in occupation of real property while depriving the claimant of rent the claimant would be entitled to in any case.

CASE STUDY 7: *BELINDA HANDSWORTH v COURTLAND MCKENZIE JR ET AL*

Introduction

The dispute involves a young man, Courtland McKenzie Jr, and a young woman, Belinda Handsworth. The two had been cohabiting for 18 months in a house legally owned by him, but in which she is claiming an equitable interest. She forced him out of the house and sued for a declaration that she was entitled to a one-half interest in it and the surrounding land; he counterclaimed for possession and damages. Soon after the legal action commenced, McKenzie Jr brought an application against Belinda Handsworth for interim payment of occupation rent. Such an application cannot be brought against a tenant by a landlord or by one spouse against another or by partners cohabiting together for two years or more. Metroland has special legislation to deal with these situations. The interim application can only be brought in a case not covered by this legislation. *Handsworth v McKenzie* was such a case.

The dispute has its roots in the couple's relationship, which started many years before in a small resort town where the two were in secondary school together. Belinda Handsworth came from an impoverished background and McKenzie Jr had a wealthy father who was opposed to their relationship. The relationship survived McKenzie Sr's disapproval and the two decided to build a house and live in it together. Belinda Handsworth is intelligent, hard working and enterprising. She is also stubborn and quick to anger. Courtland McKenzie Jr is also hard working, but passive, very much under the control and influence of his father.

The land on which the house was built belongs to McKenzie Jr. It is a valuable piece of lakeside property given to him as a gift by his father six years ago. According to McKenzie Jr, he provided all the money and some of the labour that went into the construction of the house. According to Belinda Handsworth, she contributed substantially to the project as well. She says that she was the brains of the operation and that it was her idea to build the house, now known as Sandalwood Terrace. According to Belinda, it was her planning that brought the project to fruition, and her financial contributions and attentiveness to their domestic life that enabled the project to be completed quickly and smoothly. The house was completed in May Yr–2 and the couple, still unmarried, moved in together in June Yr–2.

Their relationship has not been a happy one. According to McKenzie Jr, it is because Belinda is selfish, demanding and bad tempered. According to Belinda, the troubles between them have been instigated by McKenzie Sr who, she says, does not like her and has tried to break up the relationship. On 13 May Yr–1, after an argument and an assault by Belinda on McKenzie Jr, she ejected him from the house and changed the locks. He has not lived there since.

Shortly thereafter, in June Yr–1, McKenzie Jr executed a large mortgage against the property in favour of McKenzie Pipe Ltd, the company he works for and his father owns. Both McKenzies defend the mortgage by saying that McKenzie Jr owed much money to the company. McKenzie Jr tried to get back possession of the property, but was unable to persuade Belinda to leave even after offering her $10,000 in September Yr–1.

The offer of money to get out of the house and out of McKenzie Jr's life infuriated her. She telephoned McKenzie Sr at 3 am one morning and screamed at him.

She then sought legal advice. In October of Yr–1, she started legal action against both McKenzies and the company, Wellington Pipe Ltd. Her claim against McKenzie Jr was that, because of her contributions and his promises, she was entitled to equitable ownership in one half of the property. Her claim against all three defendants was that they had conspired to register a fraudulent mortgage against the property with the intention of depriving her of her just claims. She alleged that the loans made to McKenzie Jr by the company were a sham. They were actually employment income, disguised as loans just to avoid income tax. As a result, the mortgage given to the company was given without consideration and should be declared void and set aside. On the advice of her lawyer, she also registered a *lis pendens* against the property, thus preventing it from being mortgaged or sold until the legal action is concluded.

In late October, McKenzie Jr counterclaimed for possession of the property, occupation rent and damages for trespass and unlawful registration of the *lis pendens*. The parties' solicitors exchanged lists of documents in November Yr–1. In December, McKenzie Jr and his father went to see McKenzie Jr's lawyer, Bryan Wentworth.

Lawyers' strategies

First defendant's counsel (acting for McKenzie Jr)

My client's father, McKenzie Sr, is one of those individuals who loves a fight and loves to litigate. He has retained our firm for many years to act for him and his various companies in a wide variety of cases. He never backs down and rarely complains about the expense of litigation. When he loses, he just laughs it off. In that sense, he is the ideal client. On the other hand, because he prefers going to court rather than settling, this occasionally results in us not getting the results we wanted.

McKenzie Sr is very upset about this case, however, and he wants to find a way of settling as soon as possible. He has certainly met his match in Belinda

Handsworth. She is a young woman completely on her own, but she is ferocious, not in the least afraid of the McKenzie family, and apparently unconcerned about getting into a lawsuit against them.

In my first meeting with both McKenzies we decided that our firm should not act for all three defendants. I did not see a conflict of interest. Nevertheless, I felt that if one lawyer was acting for both McKenzies *and* the company, Belinda's lawyer could argue that there was an appearance of collusion.

McKenzie Sr initially wanted me to act for him, but because the big fight was between McKenzie Jr and Belinda, we agreed that McKenzie Sr and the company should be represented by a firm in our building, Marshall and Gavros. I would continue to act for McKenzie Jr. I made it clear that all instructions to me had to come from McKenzie Jr. McKenzie Sr seemed unmoved about this because he would call me at least once a day and try to give me instructions. After protesting several times, I finally insisted that all instructions had to be in writing signed by McKenzie Jr. Nobody seemed concerned about that. McKenzie Sr just laughed it off, getting his secretary to type the instruction letters for McKenzie Jr to sign. It does appear that Jr was not strong enough to stand up to his father. But that was something for Jr to deal with, not me.

After all, I can see Jr needs his father's support. Without it, Jr could not have tackled Belinda on his own. She is a force to be reckoned with. To both McKenzies, she presents a serious problem. She is sitting on $400,000 worth of property to the exclusion of the rightful owner. McKenzie Sr wanted to demolish the house and build an enormous condominium complex, but Belinda had tied up the property with a *lis pendens* so that nothing could be done with it. McKenzie Sr was concerned that if he did not develop the property very soon, someone else would build condominiums on the other side of the lake and beat him to it. In his view, Belinda knows this and wants to extort him into buying her out at an unreasonably high price. McKenzie Sr thinks Belinda's outrage at the $10,000 offer was staged in order to elicit a higher offer.

The McKenzies wanted me to put pressure on her. They wanted to get her into court on any pretext. They also wanted the fight resolved, but did not want to reward her bad behaviour by paying more than she legally deserved. But, as I explained to them, their options were limited. Under the Metroland CPR we could not apply for an order for sale until the extent of her interest in the property was determined at trial. We did have the option of admitting she was entitled to something, discharging the mortgage by consent and going to an assessment hearing, all of which would have meant a faster determination of the issues.

But, McKenzie Sr was against that and Jr agreed. Except for admitting that she was entitled to a limited interest in the property, the McKenzies, and Sr in particular, did not want to make any admissions on any major issue at this stage.

Under the Metroland CPR, it is also impossible for McKenzie Jr to get interim possession of the property. He does not want to move back in anyway. He is afraid of Belinda and her new boyfriend, Walter Kusyk. He does not want to live by the lake alone, isolated from his family and friends. Furthermore, even if he did return, she would still have the *lis pendens* and would be able to hold up the development of the property.

After discussing the problem with colleagues, I decided on the interim payment application, asking the court to award an interim payment of occupation rent against Belinda. The first benefit of this application was that, for my client and his father, we were doing something concrete. We were not just waiting for a trial date to be set at her convenience. There could be a delay of many months. We had to apply some pressure to push the litigation process forward and stop her from abusing it. The application itself would also compel her to pay out more money to her lawyer. A second advantage is that, if we could force her to pay something, it would make her see she could not just sit there with impunity, rent free, until trial. If she was ordered to pay a large enough sum, it could persuade her to come to terms. This would fit the McKenzies' objectives.

The risk is, if our application is unsuccessful, it could further embolden Belinda, and that would run counter to what the McKenzies wanted. The other risk is the judge might see the application as contravening r 1.1, the overriding objective of the MCPR. First, the judge might argue the application is disproportionate to the cost of making it and a waste of the court's resources. Secondly, he could view it as reinforcing financial inequality – as pressure from rich people against an impoverished young woman. Her lawyer is undoubtedly going to make that point and argue that Jr does not need the rent money now. He can afford to wait until trial. Why should the court reward him for his 'disproportionate' application by making an order against a financially weaker party?

Those are good arguments, but my approach is going to be to turn this perception on its head. I want to present Belinda as the stronger party. She may have less money, but the position she is in – suing for very little – but tying up a valuable property, makes her very strong. So strong, I shall argue, that this application is justified. If the application is successful, it will put the parties on a more equal footing by putting pressure on Belinda to settle.

The amount I am asking for in the application is relatively small. The judge will want to know why I am going to court for such a small amount. I think I should be forthright about its purpose: it is to pressure her into settling, and that is how I intend to put it. It is a gamble to be so frank about the tactics we are using, but with such an unusual application, I need to try something different. While it is true our application is tactical, given Belinda's *modus operandi*, I think it has real merit.

Claimant counsel's approach to the problem

This application is a perfect example of how an interim application can blatantly challenge the overriding objective of the MCPR. The cost of making it is disproportionate to the amount claimed. It is also reinforcing the inequality of the parties.

It is also clear the McKenzies are trying to push my client around. As soon as she threw McKenzie Jr out of the house, the three of them – father, son and company – mortgaged that property to lower her expectations. That was not a *bona fide* mortgage. My client says that the alleged loans it was intended to secure were not loans at all, but payments by Wellington Pipe Ltd to McKenzie Jr disguised as loans so that Jr would not have to pay income tax. If this can be proved at trial, the mortgage will probably be declared fraudulent and set aside.

Even if fraud cannot be proved on this application, that mortgage still looks highly suspicious. Financial chicanery such as this reveals their bullying tactics. The interim payment order is discretionary, so highlighting their bullying tactics will help to persuade the court that its discretion should not be exercised in their favour. In other words, I want to show the defendants to be manipulative schemers and bullies who should not benefit from the exercise of the court's discretion.

This approach fits well with the underlying rationale of the interim payment application. It is designed for people who are entitled to money, but cannot, or should not have to, wait for it until trial. It is usually a financially weak party asking for payment from a financially stronger party. It will not be difficult to show that McKenzie Jr and Sr have much more financial strength than Belinda and that they have no cause to ask for an interim payment order. In short, they are not only bullies, but rich bullies. Naturally, I will be more indirect when submitting this in court.

IN THE SUPREME COURT OF METROLAND

BETWEEN	**BELINDA SUSAN HANDSWORTH**	**CLAIMANT**
AND	**COURTLAND McKENZIE JR COURTLAND McKENZIE SR WELLINGTON PIPE LTD**	**DEFENDANTS**

NOTICE OF APPLICATION

Take notice that we, Bryan Wentworth and Co, solicitors on behalf of the first defendant, intend to apply, pursuant to Rules 25.1(1)(k) and 25.7(1)(d) (MCPR) for an order that the claimant (defendant by counterclaim) do make interim payment or payments to the first defendant (counterclaimant), for occupation rent in respect of the claimant's occupation of the subject property known as Sandalwood Terrace. The amounts sought for occupation rent are $15,200 arrears of rent and $1,900 per month from 1 March Yr0 until the issue of possession of the subject property is finally adjudicated.

The grounds [r 25.7 (1)(d) MCPR] on which the application is based are that:

1. the first defendant is seeking an order for possession of the subject property;

2. as the property is wholly owned by the first defendant, and is occupied solely by the claimant who has excluded the first defendant from occupation, it is highly likely that, at trial, the court will order the claimant to pay the first defendant a sum of money for occupation rent.

In support of this application, we rely on the affidavit of the first defendant Courtland McKenzie Jr, sworn on the 4th of day of January Yr0.

The time estimate for this hearing is 90 minutes which estimate has been agreed by the solicitors for the claimant.

Signed:

Brian Wentworth & Co

4 January Yr0

YR–1\7891

IN THE SUPREME COURT OF METROLAND

BETWEEN   **BELINDA SUSAN**   **CLAIMANT**
     HANDSWORTH

AND   **COURTLAND McKENZIE JR**   **DEFENDANTS**
     COURTLAND McKENZIE SR
     WELLINGTON PIPE LTD

CHRONOLOGY

3 September Yr–6   Sandalwood Terrace transferred from second defendant to first defendant

March Yr–3   Construction begins at Sandalwood Terrace

November Yr–3   Claimant and first defendant begin living together in a trailer on the construction site

May Yr–2   Occupation permit issued for Sandalwood Terrace

June Yr–2   Claimant and first defendant begin living together in Sandalwood Terrace

December Yr–2   Claimant injures first defendant with vacuum cleaner

12 May Yr–1   Claimant injures first defendant with plate

13 May Yr–1   Claimant changes locks on Sandalwood Terrace, 'throws first defendant out'

20 June Yr–1   First defendant executes and registers mortgage on Sandalwood Terrace to third defendant, Wellington Pipe Ltd

August Yr–1   Claimant begins living with Walter Kusyk at Sandalwood Terrace

12 September Yr–1   First defendant offers to pay claimant $10,000 if she vacates

15 October Yr–1	Claimant issues and serves writ and statement of claim against three defendants claiming a one-half interest in Sandalwood Terrace from the first defendant and further claiming that all three defendants conspired fraudulently to convey an interest in Sandalwood Terrace to the third defendant by mortgage.
26 October Yr–1	First defendant files defence and counterclaims for possession of Sandalwood Terrace, occupation rent, and damages for wrongful registration of *lis pendens*. Second and third defendants file defence
17 November Yr–1	Lists of documents exchanged
4 January Yr0	First defendant's solicitor issues and serves application for interim payment; first defendant executes first affidavit
13 January Yr0	Claimant's affidavit
20 January Yr0	First defendant's second affidavit

YR–1\7891

IN THE SUPREME COURT OF METROLAND

BETWEEN   **BELINDA SUSAN**   **CLAIMANT**
                     HANDSWORTH

AND   **COURTLAND McKENZIE JR**   **DEFENDANTS**
                     COURTLAND McKENZIE SR
                     WELLINGTON PIPE LTD

AFFIDAVIT

I, Courtland McKenzie Jr, plumber, of #8–1001 Imperial Close, Wellington, make oath and say as follows:

1. I am the first defendant in this action and have personal knowledge of the facts stated in this affidavit unless I have been informed by another source in which case I verily believe those facts to be true.

2. I am twenty six years old and first met the claimant in high school. The claimant, who is known as Linda, and who I shall refer to as Linda, is the same age as I am. Linda and I dated in secondary school for about two and a half years. After graduating, Linda and I broke up and I left Metroland to go to university in Ocean City. She stayed in Wellington and continued to work at the local supermarket as a cashier.

3. I did not complete university but returned to Wellington in Yr–6 at the behest of my father, Courtland McKenzie Sr, to work for him in his business. My father, who is the second defendant in this action, owns a plumbing supply business, Wellington Pipe Ltd (the third defendant), a scrap metal business, as well as several pieces of real estate, and lakefront property around Beverly Inlet outside Wellington. He is also a real estate developer and recently built a condominium development on one of his lakefront lots. I worked for him in his real estate development company for three years and then moved over to Wellington Pipe Ltd. I know my father well and, contrary to what Linda alleges in her statement of claim, he has no need or desire to defraud her of any money or assets.

4. Shortly after I returned to Wellington my father transferred to me on 3 September Yr–6, a vacant plot of lakefront property of about two and one-half acres, adjacent to the condominium development. It is that property, known as Sandalwood Terrace, which is the focal point of this legal action.

5. About a year and a half after I returned to Wellington, Linda and I started to date again. She wanted to get married, but I felt I was still too young. In addition, apart from Sandalwood Terrace, I had, and still have, virtually nothing in the way of assets. Linda insisted we get married, but I resisted until finally I agreed we could try living together. We agreed that I would build a house on Sandalwood Terrace and that we would live there. My father objected to this and told me this was not a smart thing to do because he said he could help me develop the property, build condominiums and make far more money than a house would ever make.

6. Although Linda and my father differed on this issue, she finally persuaded me that I could build the house myself which, eventually, I did. I employed an architect, but acted as my own contractor, employing sub-trades and purchasing building materials. Although my father disagreed with me over this project, he did permit me to take a great deal of time off my job to work on it. I also did a great deal of manual labour – including clearing the site, framing, painting, plumbing installation, hauling rubbish from the site, and roofing. Much help was also given by my father who provided construction crews and building materials free of charge. During this time, Linda helped a little bit, but she was too busy working at two jobs to do very much. She knew at all times that the property was mine and that my father would never have allowed her to have an interest in it. If my father had thought she considered herself to have an interest in the property, I believe he would never have given me so much help by sending his construction crew to the site. Construction began in March of Yr–3 and the house was finished in May of Yr–2, when we received an occupation permit. We had begun living together in a trailer on the site, starting in November of Yr–3. We moved into the house in June of Yr–2.

7. By the winter of Yr–2, Linda and I were having lots of conflicts. We were having constant arguments. One day in December of Yr–2, she broke my nose with the nozzle of a vacuum cleaner. I bled so profusely that I had to be hospitalised overnight. On 12 May Yr–1, she injured me again, this time by breaking a dinner plate and stabbing me with its jagged edge in the left shoulder. I drove to the hospital emergency ward myself. The doctor had to sew 13 stitches to close the wound.

8. When I returned to Sandalwood Terrace the next day, she had already changed the locks on the doors and had thrown all my personal effects on to the veranda. I had no alternative but to rent an apartment where I am paying rent of $1,250 per month.

9. Since that time, Linda has lived in the Sandalwood Terrace house by herself, except that between August and December of Yr–1 she lived there with a man named Walter Kusyk. Both I and my lawyer have sent her numerous letters asking her to vacate the house. Both the market value and the rental value of the house and land are high and she does not have my permission to live there. Attached hereto and marked exhibit A to this affidavit is a copy of a letter dated 13 December Yr–1 from Stewart Petarsky Realty to me stating the market value of Sandalwood Terrace to be between $200,000 and $400,000 depending on whether it can be rezoned for building condominiums. The rental value, according to Mr Petarsky, is approximately $2,000 per month.

10. Linda's allegation that I and my father conspired to register a fraudulent mortgage against Sandalwood Terrace is untrue. The mortgage registered against Sandalwood Terrace on 20 June Yr–1 was absolutely *bona fide*. I owed my father's company, Wellington Pipe Ltd, $98,765 because of advances the company had made to me over a three-year period. When Linda and I broke up and she would not let me back into the house I was very upset and unable to work. Wellington Pipe Ltd was naturally concerned I would be unable to pay the company back. That is why they asked me to grant the mortgage. I readily signed the mortgage document when I was asked to. As at 31 December Yr–1, the amount owing under the mortgage, including accrued interest, is $103,102. Wellington Pipe Ltd has demanded payment of the full amount.

11. On 12 September Yr–1, against my lawyer's advice, I wrote a note to Linda, a copy of which is attached as exhibit B to this affidavit, offering to pay her $10,000 if she would move out of Sandalwood Terrace. Her response to this offer was to telephone my parents' house at 3 am. She woke up my mother who is ill with phlebitis and spoke to my father. I was informed by my father that she was screaming and cursing my father and me, using foul language. Her next response was to start a lawsuit. She brought two legal actions against me, one claiming a one-half interest in Sandalwood Terrace and the other against me, my father and his company claiming that we conspired to register a fraudulent mortgage against Sandalwood Terrace to the third defendant, Wellington Pipe Ltd. Notwithstanding her reaction to my offer, it remains open.

12. For the last several months I have been unable to make the payments on this mortgage and Wellington Pipe Ltd has been indulgent enough not to start foreclosure proceedings, although they have threatened to do so. My father has also offered to buy back Sandalwood Terrace from me; however, because Linda has brought legal action and registered a *lis pendens* against the property, I am unable to sell it. In addition, since living there has been made impossible for me I am being deprived of its occupation value as well.

13. Attached as exhibit C to this affidavit is a document entitled 'Occupation rent calculations', which sets out the method by which I calculate the amount of occupation rent I am seeking in this application.

14. In the circumstances, I respectfully request this honourable court to order the claimant to pay to me by way of interim payment a reasonable amount for occupation rent as set out in exhibit C.

Sworn before me in the City of Metrocity

on the 4th day of January Yr0

Timothy Maitland   C McKenzie

Commissioner for taking Affidavits in Metroland

Stewart Petarsky Realty
329 Trellis Road
Wellington 2025

Tel: 487 2784 Fax: 487 2780
Cell: 801 3278 e-mail: spetarsky@metrocan.com
www.petarskyrealty.com

13 December, Yr—1

Mr Courtland McKenzie Jr
#8—1001 Imperial Close
Wellington

Dear Cortie,

Re: Lakeside Property 'Sandalwood Terrace'

At your request, I have inspected the above property and looked at comparative sales in the area. As you know, Linda Handsworth would not permit me to enter the house but, with your assistance, I was able to look at the interior through the many large size windows.

This is a unique lakeside property with beautiful views of Lake Wellington, nearly three acres of forested land, and an accessible, if rocky beach. The frame house is newly built, with double-glazed windows, oak floors, stone façade, fireplace, and new appliances. According to the architect's plans that I have seen, the interior of the house is approximately 2,500 square feet. It has three bedrooms, sitting room, dining room, kitchen, two three-piece bathrooms and a large veranda built round the perimeter of the house that provides views of the lake in front and views of White Wolf Mountain in the rear. Part of the veranda at the back has a functioning three-person jacuzzi. I understand there is also a sauna on the first floor. Water is provided by well and sewage is drained into a septic tank.

It is difficult to compare this to other properties because of its uniqueness. For market purposes, it is essentially a vacation home and would not appeal to most Wellington residents as a permanent home because it is too far from schools and other services. On that basis and on the basis of comparison to other 'sold' houses in the area, I would say it should be listed at about $215,000 and will probably sell at around $200,000. If it is listed for sale nearer the summer months I foresee that much more interest will be generated. I have no comment on whether or not it can be rezoned, except to say that if a rezoning application is successful, the land value will undoubtedly be worth considerably more than $200,000. A quick guess would be $400,000.

Because it is close to White Wolf Mountain and on the Lake, its rental value during the ski and summer seasons is high. For four to five months a year, it could be as high as $5,000 per month. However, during the remainder of the year it is much lower, perhaps as low as $1,000 per month if tenants can be found — which is not always easy. On average, I would estimate the monthly rental value for the whole year to be approximately $2,000 per month.

I hope this information is helpful to you. If I can be of further assistance please give me a call.

Sincerely,

S Petarsky

This is exhibit A to the affidavit of Courtland McKenzie Jr sworn herein on the 4th day of January Yr0 in Metrocity.

Timothy Maitland

Commissioner for taking Affidavits in Metroland

12/09/Yr-1

Linda,

Let's clean up this mess once and for all and stop torturing one another. I still love you, but we can't live together any more. We're still young and can start new lives.

Besides, it is not fair for you to live at Sandalwood Terrace while I have to pay rent elsewhere. You have to leave and let me live there or sell it back to Dad for development.

I'll pay you $10,000 cash but you must give up on Sandalwood Terrace and move out. We can still be friends. OK?

Call me,

Cortie

This is exhibit B to the affidavit of Courtland McKenzie Jr sworn herein on the 4th day of January Yr0 in Metrocity

Timothy Maitland

Commissioner for taking Affidavits in Metroland

Occupation rent calculations

Present market value of Sandalwood Terrace

$200,000

Estimate of Ms Handsworth's contributions to the value of the property to date

November Yr–3 [month she began to live on the site] to May Yr–2 [house completed]: 7 months

Estimate of monthly contribution in cash and labour: $1,000

Total estimated contribution: 7 x $1,000 = $7,000 or 3.5 % of market value

Add another $3,000 for margin of error and the total is $10,000 or 5% of market value

Occupation rent payable to Mr McKenzie Jr

If Ms Handsworth is entitled to 5% of market value, then 95% is attributable to Mr McKenzie Jr

If the market rent is $2,000 per month, the amount attributable to Mr McKenzie Jr should be 95% x $2,000, or $1,900

Ms Handsworth has been in occupation to the exclusion of Mr McKenzie Jr from June Yr–1 to date [February Yr0] or 8 months

Rent arrears are 8 x $1,900 = $15,200

Comparison of estimated claims against each other

McKenzie Jr claims occupation rent of approximately $15,200 plus $1,900 per month

Ms Handsworth claims a contribution of about $10,000

[The above figures are used for the purposes of argument and are not intended to constitute evidence or admissions.]

This is exhibit C to the affidavit of Courtland McKenzie Jr sworn herein on the 4th day of January Yr0 in Metrocity

Timothy Maitland

Commissioner for taking Affidavits in Metroland

IN THE SUPREME COURT OF METROLAND

BETWEEN   **BELINDA SUSAN**   **CLAIMANT**
               HANDSWORTH

AND   **COURTLAND McKENZIE JR**   **DEFENDANTS**
           COURTLAND McKENZIE SR
           WELLINGTON PIPE LTD

AFFIDAVIT

I, Belinda Susan Handsworth, store clerk, of Rural Route 4 (Sandalwood Terrace), Beverly Inlet, Wellington, make oath and say as follows:

1. I am the claimant in this action and have personal knowledge of the facts stated in this affidavit unless informed by another person in which case I verily believe those facts to be true.

2. I have read the affidavit of Courtland McKenzie Jr (whom I shall refer to as Cortie) dated the 4th day of January Yr0 and respond as follows:

3. I have known the claimant all my life as we grew up together in Wellington. Although not in the same classes, we did go to the same primary school. I noticed him even then because everyone knew he was the son of the mayor of Wellington, Courtland McKenzie Sr ('Mr McKenzie'). It appears from what Cortie has said, however, that he only noticed me in secondary school. We started to go out together in our first year and remained close throughout secondary school.

4. By our final year, the relationship had become quite serious. Observing this, Cortie's father, Mr McKenzie, strongly objected to Cortie and I going out together. I once overheard him refer to me as 'the cleaning woman's daughter'. Cortie told me that Mr McKenzie had once said that my late father was not my real father, but a transient who had passed through our town. Comments such as this, which I knew were malicious and untrue, wounded me deeply. When Cortie's father sent him away to university in Yr–8 to break up the relationship, a part of me was relieved to see the relationship come to an end, but I was still heartbroken to say goodbye to Cortie.

5. After graduation, I found a job at Greenway's Superstore and worked at night at Ray's Pub.

6. In Yr–5, Cortie, who had returned to Wellington and was working for his father, began coming around to Greenway's and asking me out again. I did not want to go out with him because I knew his family would object and treat me badly. But he persisted. On our first date, he asked me to marry him. I agreed on one condition – that he get out from under his father's thumb and do something on his own. He agreed that he would. As events unfolded, however, Cortie was never able to escape from his father's clutches. This was the fundamental problem of our relationship and it was my mistake to believe that Cortie could do anything on his own. In Yr–4, however, I did not yet realise this and pressed him to get married and start a business with me.

7. But Cortie felt, as he said to me many times, that he could not give up his job with his father yet. He needed time to persuade his father that our marriage would be good. So we compromised. We agreed to build a house together, without Mr McKenzie's help, at Lake Wellington. At first, Mr McKenzie objected, but then he saw that there wasn't much he could do to stop it. Cortie managed to stand firm against his father's objections and, for the first time in our lives together, I could see he felt good about himself. We agreed that after the house was finished we would live together in it and then get married. We agreed that we would both work on building the house and that half of it would be mine.

8. The serious problems in our relationship began when Cortie's father realised that Cortie and I were going ahead to build the house without him. It started when I employed the architect, Bryan Delvecchio, to do drawings. That is when his father employed another better known architect to do new drawings. After I refused this new architect's 'help', Mr McKenzie started sending over building materials and a construction crew. I wanted to pay for the materials and send the crew back but Cortie disagreed with me and persuaded me to accept his father's help.

9. Soon after we started living together in Sandalwood Terrace, Cortie would not, as we had agreed, leave his job and start a business with me. He was afraid to make the change and kept pointing out how generous his father could be and how he had helped to build the house. This, I admit, made me angry.

10. In response to para 6 of Cortie's affidavit , it is false and misleading for him to say that we agreed that 'he' would build the house, and it is false and misleading for him not to acknowledge my

contributions to the project. The fact is, I initiated and managed the whole project. While it is true that Cortie paid the architect, and the sub-trades, I conceived the basic design, selected the architect to put it on paper and submitted the plans to the City Council with him. In October of Yr–3, Cortie asked me to move into his trailer on the construction site so that we could work continuously on it and so that I could take care of him while he worked on it. I cleaned and redecorated the trailer. I did all the food shopping, nearly all the meal making and all the laundry, thus freeing Cortie to work on the house. I paid all the fuel, electricity and telephone bills. At that time, Cortie had very few responsibilities on the construction site except manual labour. But I also worked hard on the house. I worked on weekends and on holidays, clearing land, framing, hammering, dry walling, pouring concrete, ordering materials, hauling rubbish, finishing, sanding, painting and directing the workmen and Cortie.

11. By the end of Yr–2, Cortie fell increasingly under his father's spell again. He felt he could not give up his job with his father. He often did not come home until late in the evening after going out drinking with his father and his friends. He told me his father said he was going to retire soon and hand over the business to him. When I tried to talk to him he would wave me away. I admit I broke his nose with a vacuum cleaner nozzle as alleged in para 7 of his affidavit, but this was accidental. As I was vacuuming, we were arguing. He grabbed me from behind, I tried to break free and my hand, holding the nozzle, struck his face.

12. The stabbing on 12 May Yr–1, however, also referred to in para 7 of Cortie's affidavit, was not accidental. On that day, I told him I thought I was pregnant because I had conducted a home pregnancy test and it had produced a positive result. He told me his father was right, I was trying to 'trap' him and I 'better get an abortion if I knew what was good for' me. That comment made me very angry. I threw a plate at him. He threw a broken piece of it at my face very close to my left eye. I picked up the piece of plate and stabbed him in the shoulder with it. When he left the house I threw all his things out the front door, called the locksmith and had the locks changed. Later, after conducting a second pregnancy test, I discovered I was not pregnant.

13. In mid-September of Yr–1, I received a telephone call from Cortie. He had just written me a note offering me $10,000 if I would move out of Sandalwood Terrace. He told me he owed his father a lot of money and had mortgaged the house in June so he could pay it back. When I questioned him about the money he owed, he said that most of it was for loans the company had given him and some of it

was for building materials that Wellington Pipe Ltd had supplied to 'build the house'.

14. I was naturally furious. What about all the time I had put in? I said. What about the night job I had kept? What about all the time I had helped and supported him? I protested that all the building materials were supposed to be gifts from his father. Furthermore, I protested, how dare his father say that Cortie owed money to Wellington Pipe Ltd? That was an accounting trick. Cortie told me that most of the money he received from the company was in the form of 'loans to director', that is, cash paid to Cortie as a director that he is supposed to pay back or is obliged to pay back, but never actually pays back. Cortie told me that the purpose of arranging his finances in this way is for him to have the benefit of not paying income tax. Even the company accountant, Jackie McKenzie, once told me that she doubted if the so called director's loans to Cortie would ever have to be paid back. They were called 'loans' just to avoid income taxes. That night I could not sleep and was so angry I did call his father as alleged in para 11 of Cortie's affidavit. I did shout at him, but did not use foul language as alleged. Attached as exhibit A to this affidavit is a copy of the 'Advances to director – C McKenzie Jr' account supplied by Wellington Pipe Ltd to my lawyer.

15. Attached and marked exhibit B to this affidavit is a letter from my lawyer dated 4 December Yr–1 to the lawyer for the second and third defendants, Mr McKenzie and Wellington Pipe Ltd. On my instructions, my lawyer, Mr Temple, wrote this letter for the purpose of requesting further documents in relation to my claim for fraudulent conveyance. Mr Temple has informed me that he has received no reply to this letter.

16. I oppose the application for interim payment. Cortie has far more financial resources than I do. He can draw funds from the third defendant at any time and has unlimited support from his father. I have total savings of approximately $35,000 and an income from two jobs of $3,200 per month before taxes.

Sworn before me in the City of Metrocity

on the 13th day of January Yr0

VG Petrocelli   Belinda Handsworth

Commissioner for taking Affidavits in Metroland

Wellington Pipe Ltd

Advances to director – C McKenzie Jr	Debit	Credit	Balance
8 Feb Yr–3	1,276.00		
28 April	2,313.00		
14 May	4,100.00		
28 August	2,699.00		
2 Sept	1,987.00		
20 Dec	5,000.00		
12 Feb Yr–2	5,600.00		
16 May	5,800.00		
28 June	6,086.00		
2 August	2,341.00		
28 August	1,187.00		
9 Dec	3,900.00		
23 Feb Yr–1	4,160.65		
30 March	1,200.00		
12 April	12,367.78		
21 May	11,267.57		
3 June	9,500.00		
17 June	17,980.00		98,765.00

**This is exhibit A to the affidavit of Belinda Susan Handsworth
sworn on 13 January Yr0 at Metrocity**

VG Petrocelli

Commissioner for taking Affidavits in Metroland

Blaise Temple and Weiler
Barristers and Solicitors
16th Floor Lloyd-Packard Centre
Metrocity
Metroland 4926
Tel: (610) 693 3790 Fax: (610) 693 8871
e-mail: btwlawyers@lawpool.met.me

Reply to: Leonard Temple
Tel: (610) 693 3795
e-mail:ltemple@lawpool.met.me
4 December Yr–1

Your file no: Fwt–20039
Our file no: Lfdom/742
Marshall and Gavros
Barristers and Solicitors
1 Franklin Walk
Metrocity, 4926

Attention: Ms Felicity Walker-Chow   **BY FAX AND POST**

Dear Sirs/Mesdames,

<u>Handsworth v McKenzie et al</u>

We wish to note as a matter of record as a follow up to our telephone conversation that, although you have provided us with a list of documents, that list does not include all statements of account and entries of account of Wellington Pipe Ltd ('the company') that relate to any and all payments or loans made to the younger McKenzie for the last three years, commencing 1 January Yr–3 to date, and any and all payments or loans made by him to the company in the same period, all cancelled cheques in relation thereto, and all loan agreements made between the company and the younger McKenzie. The only account documents relevant to our claim for fraudulent conveyance that you have listed – and that we have now seen – are a copy of the mortgage, already publicly available in the land registry and the loan account showing loan advances to the younger McKenzie. This second document is on one sheet of paper and appears to be a summary of alleged 'advances'. In relation to that document, we need to see all original entries of account, and cancelled cheques supporting those entries. We also request production of your client's income tax returns for the last three years. Please amend your list of documents accordingly and let us know when these documents can be inspected.

Sincerely yours,

L Temple

Leonard Temple

cc Mr Bryan Wentworth

This is exhibit B to the affidavit of Belinda Susan Handsworth sworn on 13 January Yr0 at Metrocity

VG Petrocelli

_____

Commissioner for taking Affidavits in Metroland

BETWEEN   **BELINDA SUSAN**   **CLAIMANT**
HANDSWORTH

AND   **COURTLAND McKENZIE JR**   **DEFENDANTS**
COURTLAND McKENZIE SR
WELLINGTON PIPE LTD

AFFIDAVIT

I, Courtland McKenzie Jr, plumber, of #8–1001 Imperial Close, Wellington, make oath and say as follows:

1. I am the first defendant in this action and have personal knowledge of the facts deposed to except where the same are stated to be on information and belief and where so stated I verily believe them to be true.

2. I have read the affidavit of Belinda Susan Handsworth dated 13 January Yr–1. I shall reply to only a few of these allegations here. I have been advised by my lawyer that most of the allegations are inflammatory and not relevant to this application. I do not wish further to inflame the dispute between the claimant and me by answering all the allegations. I reserve the right to dispute these allegations before or at trial if it is necessary or becomes relevant.

3. In response to para 7 and 8 of the claimant's affidavit, I never agreed that half the Sandalwood Terrace house would be the claimant's.

4. In further response to para 7 and 8 the money advanced to me by Wellington Pipe Ltd referred to in exhibit B to the claimant's affidavit was a *bona fide* loan from that company, much of it going to pay sub-contractors hired to build Sandalwood Terrace. I must pay it back and, in fact, the company has demanded I do so. I deny that this arrangement has anything to do with income tax as alleged.

5. In response to para 8, the claimant did not refuse my father's help. On the contrary, she welcomed it.

6. In response to para 10, Linda did a very minimal amount of work on the house. I also took a great deal more responsibility than just manual labour. For example, I drew the plans for the installation of the septic tank and the digging of the well. I selected and supervised the sub-trades. I

liaised with the architect and I handled all disputes between the sub-trades. I handled all the finances and paid all bills related to the building of the house. While it is true that Linda purchased some of the groceries, I never declined to pay any bills she presented to me.

7. In response to para 16, I deny that I can draw money at any time from the third defendant or have unlimited support from my father.

Sworn before me in the City of Metrocity
on the 20th day of January Yr0

Timothy Maitland   *C McKenzie*
_____

Commissioner for taking Affidavits in Metroland

Oral submissions by counsel

First defendant counsel's submission	Page ref
If it please your Lordship, my name is Bryan Wentworth and I appear on behalf of the first defendant, Courtland McKenzie Jr. Appearing on behalf of the claimant is Mr Leonard Temple. On behalf of the second and third defendants is Ms Felicity Walker-Chow.	
Judge: It's your application, then, Mr Wentworth?	
First defendant's counsel: Yes it is, my Lord. Mr Temple for the claimant is opposing. Ms Walker-Chow for the other two defendants and I have had discussions this morning and she has indicated to me that she will probably make no submissions.	
Judge [*looking at Ms Walker-Chow*]: Is that right?	
Second and third defendant's counsel: That is basically right, my Lord. We've been served, but take no position except that my clients take strong objection to the allegations of fraud. My clients have an excellent reputation in the Wellington area and the claimant should know that baseless allegations of fraud will be vigorously resisted. Should claimant's counsel try to argue the issue of fraud on this application, I shall have to respond. Otherwise, I doubt a response from me will be necessary.	
Judge [*to Ms Walker-Chow*]: The claimant has sued your clients for fraudulent conveyance. They want to set aside the company's mortgage. So they are definitely not on the claimant's side. Is that fair to say?	
Second and third defendant's counsel: Yes it is, my Lord.	
Judge: And she's sued Mr McKenzie Jr for the same thing alleging what amounts to a conspiracy between all three defendants. She is also suing for a declaration she's entitled to a half-interest in the property. Is that right?	
Second and third defendant's counsel: Right, my Lord.	
Judge: All right. Mr Wentworth, I've read all the material including your chronology. Proceed with your application.	

First defendant's counsel: My Lord, this is an application on behalf of the first defendant, Courtland McKenzie Jr, for an order pursuant to Part 25 of the Civil Procedure Rules and specifically Rule 25.7(1)(d). We are asking that the respondent on this application, Belinda Handsworth, pay to the first defendant an interim payment or payments for occupation rent in relation to a house and land she is occupying known as Sandalwood Terrace. The house and land belong to the first defendant. They are registered in his name. His father, the second defendant, gave the property to him as a gift six years ago.

156

We are seeking occupation rent for the period beginning 13 May Yr–1 – which is the date the claimant changed the locks on the doors and removed the first defendant's belongings from the house – until trial, the date for which has not yet been fixed. The first defendant has not lived there since the locks were changed, although he has tried several times to persuade the claimant to vacate the property so that he could retake possession.

157

My Lord, the court's authority to make an order for interim payment is contained in Part 25. According to Order 25.7(1)(d), the court can make an order for interim payment in relation to occupation rent if the applicant meets two preconditions:

First, the applicant must be seeking an order for possession of land. We obviously meet this precondition, my Lord: the first defendant's counterclaim does seek an order for possession of Sandalwood Terrace.

The second precondition is that the applicant should be able to show that if the case went to trial, the respondent would be held liable to pay occupation rent while the claim for possession was pending.

My Lord, we also meet this precondition. The respondent on this application, Ms Handsworth, is claiming, at most, a one-half interest in Sandalwood Terrace. Since 13 May of last year, she has been occupying the property to the exclusion of the owner/applicant, Courtland McKenzie Jr. If this case goes to trial and Ms Handsworth is successful in proving she is entitled to a one-half interest, she will still be obliged to pay occupation rent to Courtland McKenzie for his half of the property. I do not think my learned friend will be suggesting any defence to this claim for occupation rent.

157

So, my Lord, in view of the fact that we meet both preconditions for this application, I shall go on to propose an appropriate payment structure for the payment of occupation rent in these circumstances.

First off, my Lord, I should emphasise that Ms Handsworth's claim to one-half the property is a very doubtful one. On equitable principles well known to this court, I do not believe that she could seriously argue that her contribution is anywhere near 50%. She says that Mr McKenzie Jr said she would get 50%, but this is something he flatly denies. In any event, even if he did say something like this, or acquiesce in something she said, it needs to be seen in the context of two young people talking about a future together and not in the context of contractual discussions.

My Lord, even Ms Handsworth's affidavit confirms the view that the discussions between these two young people were about marriage. If one wanted to use legal terminology to describe these discussions, one could say that whatever promises were made, if any, were conditional on marriage taking place – which it has not done. There has been no marriage here. This is not a matrimonial property claim. My Lord, if I can refer you to Ms Handsworth's affidavit, para 7. If I can bring you down to the last three lines: 'We agreed that after the house was finished we would live together in it and then get married. We agreed that we would both work on building the house and that half of it would be mine.'

My Lord, they were to be married first, after which – over time – they would acquire rights to each other's property. That is what the law of this country provides and that is most probably the gist of what Mr McKenzie Jr was saying – if in fact he used the words Ms Handsworth said he used. The conclusion to be drawn from this, my Lord, is that any promises alleged to have been made by Mr McKenzie Jr to Ms Handsworth are unlikely to affect the court's ultimate finding of how much of the Sandalwood Terrace property she is entitled to.

My Lord, unless I can assist you further in elaborating the first point, I will proceed to deal with quantifying the extent of her entitlement.

What would affect her entitlement?

168

The amount of her actual contribution in relation to Mr McKenzie's contribution. Clearly, his contribution is very large and hers is very, very small. I shall summarise those contributions on the basis of the information available in the affidavits:

1   He contributed nearly all the money that went into the construction of the house.

2   He contributed a great deal of his own labour, taking time off work.   160

3   She contributed some labour to the planning and construction of the house, but took no time off work. [During the preparation and construction of the house, Ms Handsworth maintained both her jobs which took up most of her time.]   160

4   Arguably, she made a small indirect contribution through purchases of groceries, payment of bills, and meal preparation.   175

5   Finally, most of the value is in the land itself, all of which he contributed. If the land is valued for development – if it is rezoned – it is worth $400,000. And if the land is rezoned the house will be demolished.   163–64

My Lord, given these facts, it must be fair to say it would be very unlikely that Ms Handsworth would be able to prove a sizeable contribution, if any.

My Lord, if I can refer you to the document titled 'Occupation rent calculations'. It is attached as exhibit C to Mr McKenzie   166
Jr's first affidavit. That document sets out Ms Handsworth's estimated contributions to Sandalwood Terrace and some figures showing how I submit occupation rent should be calculated. Can I invite your Lordship to look at that exhibit for a moment or two?

Judge: Yes, thank you. [*Reads and then looks up.*]

First defendant's counsel: Even if we say, for example, that she was on the site for seven months, from November Yr–3 to May Yr–2, and we say further that her contribution was around $1,000 per month in labour and indirect contributions, this is only a $7,000 contribution which is less than Mr McKenzie Jr offered her and only 3.5% of the present market value of Sandalwood Terrace, which is $200,000. To give her the benefit of the doubt, let us say the upper limit of her entitlement, if any, might be 5% of market value. This amounts to only $10,000. I should stress here, my Lord, that my client has offered Ms Handsworth $10,000 to settle this entire matter and has instructed me to leave this offer open indefinitely. That is why, for the purposes of argument, we have raised her hypothetical interest from 3.5% to 5%.

My Lord, logic dictates that the occupation rent payable to Mr McKenzie Jr should be 95% of the market rent. Market rent is, according to Mr Petarsky's letter, $2,000 per month. So, 95% of $2,000 is $1,900. My Lord, Ms Handsworth has been in occupation since May of Yr–1. It is now February, Yr0. If we count from June until January, she has been in occupation for eight months. Eight times $1,900 is $15,200. Therefore, she is already in arrears in the amount of $15,200 and each month she owes Mr McKenzie Jr a further $1,900.

If your Lordship were to grant our application in full, then you could order an interim payment of $15,000 and a further payment of $1,900 per month each month commencing immediately.

Nevertheless, My Lord, under Order 25.7(4) and (5) your Lordship must not order an interim payment of more than a reasonable proportion of the likely amount of the final judgment and your Lordship does need to take into account counterclaims or set offs – in this case, Ms Handsworth's claim for an interest in the property.

Based on the figures I have provided to your Lordship, our claim for occupation rent is probably a good deal larger than Ms Handsworth's claim for an interest in the property: $15,200 versus approximately $10,000. The difference is approximately $5,000.

My Lord, I suggest an immediate payment of $5,000 and a monthly rental payment of $1,000 per month. My Lord ...

Judge: Mr Wentworth, let me stop you right there. What are we doing here in court arguing about $5,000? Does a claim for occupation rent in that amount justify an interim application? The legal costs for just one party will be larger than that. This looks to me like a complete waste of the court's resources. Is this dealing with a case 'proportionately' as described in Rule 1.1?

First defendant's counsel: I am indebted to your Lordship for raising this issue, because it brings us to the crux of this whole case, which is this: the claimant has brought a lawsuit in Supreme Court over what is unlikely to be more than $10,000. It is actually likely to be less, and she may not get anything at all. And yet, my Lord, if this legal action involved only $10,000, we would not be here. The first defendant would not be bringing this application. But, because of the way the claimant has conducted herself, there is much more at stake here than $10,000.

The claimant controls property that could be worth as much as $400,000 – against which she has a claim for less than $10,000. Yet, she has tied up the property with a *lis pendens* and has ejected the first defendant from his home. He cannot live there; he cannot sell it; he cannot do a thing with it until the trial and we cannot say with certainty when that will be. It seems to the first defendant grossly unfair that the claimant should be able to control his only asset without paying anything for using and enjoying it and with absolute impunity for tying it up.

My Lord, he has offered to pay her $10,000 to settle this dispute and I submit that is more than fair. But this claimant is an angry young woman and, for her, fairness seems not to be the issue.

If I can trouble your Lordship to refer to her affidavit, the second page. If I can bring your Lordship down to para 9. She says: 'This, I admit, made me angry.' If we can move down to para 12, 'That comment made me very angry.' Paragraph 14, 'I was naturally furious'. Further down in para 14, 'That night I could not sleep and was so angry I did call his father ...'. My Lord, when she broke his nose with a vacuum cleaner, stabbed him with a shard from a broken plate, threw his things out the front door, and called Mr McKenzie Sr in the middle of the night, I daresay she must also have been quite angry. And, obviously, she is still very angry.

Even after the offer of $10,000 was put on the table, she showed no sign of an inclination to negotiate. There was no counter offer, not even an invitation to sit down and talk. The claimant is either too angry or in too strong a position to feel any pressure whatsoever to make any move. Perhaps if she had to pay something – just a little – for the benefit she is receiving she may begin to see this dispute from a more

168
169
170

169

realistic angle. She is angry and may have every right to feel angry for what has occurred between her and Mr McKenzie Jr. But, my Lord, I submit that using the legal system to channel her anger is not what this system is for. What she is doing, my Lord, is in fact abuse of process or something very close to it. I submit to your Lordship that the courts should not encourage this in any way. An order for the payment of occupation rent would positively discourage it. It could bring both parties to the bargaining table and produce a quick end to this action.

My Lord, unless I can clarify any further points, those are my submissions.

Judge: Thank you, Mr Wentworth. Mr Temple?

Claimant counsel's submission

Claimant's counsel: My Lord, I was quite intrigued by what my learned friend said toward the end of his submission. I took a note of it. If I understood him correctly, he said that the claimant doesn't feel any pressure to settle and that an interim order for payment of occupation rent could very well achieve that purpose – that is to say, pressure her into settling.

With respect, my Lord, this is the first time I have heard it argued that the purpose of an interim payment application is to pressure people into settling. I was always under the impression that the main purpose of an interim payment application is to alleviate the burden of those who have to wait a long time to obtain money damages or other remedies for wrongs done. People injured in accidents who have claims likely to be successful need money to get treatment or to tide them over during periods of unemployment owing to their injuries. In these situations, an interim payment is an indispensable and just remedy.

Now, my Lord, I am not saying this application is the same as one involving a claim in damages for personal injury. Far from it. Nevertheless, there are similarities, one of which is that all interim payment orders are discretionary, and in exercising its discretion, the court needs to apply the overriding objective of the Rules, which is to deal with cases justly. In doing so, it should take into account, among other things, the financial position of the parties as well as the principle of ensuring the parties are on an equal footing.

Now, my Lord, it seems to me that the party applying for the interim payment in this case is suffering from no financial hardship whatsoever. On the contrary, the evidence shows that, compared to the claimant, he has very considerable resources indeed. My Lord, the claimant says Mr McKenzie Jr can draw on as much money as he needs from the third defendant, Wellington Pipe Ltd. Mr McKenzie Jr has denied this, but there is evidence that seems to suggest otherwise.

My Lord, if I can refer your Lordship to exhibit A of the claimant's affidavit, the account document headed up with 'Wellington Pipe Ltd'. This document, which purports to record advances to Mr McKenzie Jr, was provided to us on discovery by Wellington Pipe Ltd, the third defendant. What is noteworthy about this document, my Lord, is that it shows a consistent, if not completely regular, pattern of payments to Mr McKenzie Jr over a period of three years. Last year, the sums drawn amounted to $56,476, which is more than half of the total of all sums drawn. This is quite remarkable, my Lord, since the entries for last year only go up to June on this document. One wonders how much he drew out during the second half of Yr–1.

171

My Lord, there also seems to be no evidence of the terms of repayment, if indeed there are any terms at all.

Also a mystery is the full extent of Mr McKenzie Jr's resources, which have not been revealed. This may only be the tip of the iceberg. My Lord, I again refer you to the claimant's affidavit. If I can bring you to the letter from our firm dated 4 December Yr–1 attached as exhibit B. In that letter I requested documents that might shed light on Mr McKenzie's resources. I have not received a reply.

172

Judge: I don't see the relevance. I don't see why you are entitled to get financial information from the first defendant. This is a trust action, not a matrimonial action.

Claimant's counsel: Your Lordship is quite right. Whether or not we can get the financial information we have requested is not an issue on this application. It will be an issue if we need to apply to compel production of that information. My Lord, the reason I am raising the issue in this way is merely to point out that Mr McKenzie Jr's financial resources appear to be very substantial and, though we have asked him to clarify the extent of those resources, he has not yet done so. I should add, he has not done so in his affidavit either.

Of course, my Lord, he does not have to do so; there is no law that says he must. But if he does not, then surely your Lordship is entitled to draw the inference that his resources are indeed substantial. At the very least, given that he has claimed no financial hardship in his affidavit, your Lordship should be able safely to infer that he could make do very nicely without occupation rent.

My Lord, the first defendant is not a typical interim payment applicant in need of a cash infusion to keep his legal action going. If he were, he could not have afforded to bring an application such as this one. As your Lordship has already pointed out, the potential gain from this application is disproportionately small when compared to the cost of bringing it. For this reason, my Lord, this application runs counter to Rule 1.1.

My Lord, if I may, I would like to conclude by suggesting another reason why it runs counter to Rule 1.1: it is trying to put the parties on an *un*equal footing, not an equal footing as is required. It is trying to browbeat the claimant with even more financial pressure. The fact is, the financial strength of the defendants obviously overmatches that of the claimant by a wide margin. The gap in their relative wealth – or, at least, the perceived gap – is one of the sources of their conflict. What my learned friend has suggested, however, is that because the claimant has a *lis pendens* registered against the property and is living in it, both of which she has an absolute right to, she is the bully and the first defendant is the victim. All the financial pressure is on him and none is on her. She's in the driver's seat and he is an unwilling passenger. So now she needs some pressure to settle. That is the way my learned friend has put his argument.

My Lord, I respectfully submit that the reverse is true. The pressure – and the financial ability to exert it – comes from the defendants' side. This application is only one manifestation of it. A more telling one is what the defendants were doing in May and June of last year.

My Lord, if I can ask your Lordship to refer again to exhibit A of the claimant's affidavit. If I may, my Lord, I'd like to bring you down to the last three entries, namely, 21 May, 3 June and

17 June of Yr–1. Except for 12 April, these are by far the three largest amounts of money drawn down by the first defendant, Mr McKenzie Jr. They indicate advances to him of a total of $38,747. I ask your Lordship to note that these three advances all took place shortly after Mr McKenzie Jr departed Sandalwood Terrace and within a short time before the mortgage was registered against the property. My Lord, if you wouldn't mind referring to the Chronology.

171

157

Your Lordship can see from the Chronology that the first defendant moved out on 13 May. It was after the 13th, but before the registration of the mortgage, that the large sums of money were advanced.

Now, the claimant is saying that the mortgage is fraudulent, given without consideration, and designed to reduce the first defendant's equity in the property. We have not proved that yet, my Lord. That is for trial.

Nevertheless, fraudulent or not, I submit that this transaction is a transparently high pressure tactic exerted by the defendants on the claimant at a very critical time – shortly after the first defendant moved out of the property. That transaction communicated to the claimant that whatever her expectations of her rights might be, they could be quickly and easily dashed by the McKenzie family with a clever manoeuvre. Your Lordship would not be stretching the facts to infer that the McKenzie family knew that the claimant had some rights, and might soon try to exercise them. That's when they arranged that mortgage. This, my Lord, was the biggest, most provocative and most unequal application of pressure in this case. I submit that allowing the first defendant to exert even more would defeat the purpose of the Rules. I therefore urge Your Lordship not to grant the application for interim payment.

My Lord, unless I can assist further, those are my submissions.

First defendant counsel's reply

Judge: Thank you, Mr Temple. Mr Wentworth. Reply?

First defendant's counsel: Thank you, my Lord. I have just two points to make. There are instances in which one party may be financially stronger, but the other has a distinct and powerful advantage because of a peculiarity in the law – so much of an advantage that there is no incentive for that party to act reasonably, no incentive whatsoever to talk about settling. In this case, the peculiarity in the law is that even if a claimant has a relatively tiny equitable claim to property, she can still tie it up with a *lis pendens*, and she can live in it without being vulnerable to an interim possession application. If the parties were married, the first defendant would be able to apply for interim possession. But they aren't married, so he cannot apply and he cannot apply for an order for sale either.

What the first defendant is seeking to do, I submit, is consistent with Rule 1.1. Rule 1.1 does not say 'equal 'financial' footing'. It just says that, in doing justice, the court must try to ensure parties are on an 'equal footing'. The first defendant is not trying to browbeat the claimant. The claimant will still be liable for occupation rent, no matter what occurs – even if the mortgage is set aside as fraudulent. My learned friend has never argued, and could not argue, that the claimant would not be liable for occupation rent. The first defendant is simply trying to get the claimant to pay that rent now so as to equalise their positions. In this way, hopefully, she will have some incentive to settle.

Which brings me to my last point. My Lord, I submit there is nothing wrong with encouraging the parties to settle by using an interim application. The new regime and the thrust of the Rules are quite clear on this. The old regime was perhaps less clear. Interim applications, however, have always been used to create pressure to settle. Perhaps one difference between the old regime and the new is that, under the new, perhaps it will become customary to say explicitly that pressure to settle is the purpose of the application. As long as the application is properly brought, my Lord, I submit that this is an appropriate and worthwhile purpose. I urge Your Lordship to grant the application with an order in terms.

Judge: Ms Walker-Chow? Do you have anything to add?

Counsel for the second and third defendants: My learned friend, Mr Wentworth, has ably and succinctly put forward all arguments. I have nothing to add, my Lord.

Outcome

Mr Wentworth's strategy, which was to argue that the claimant, Ms Handsworth, was in a stronger position than the first defendant despite the first defendant's ample resources, did not succeed. An extract from the judge's decision set out below explains why:

Judge: ... the claimant's case claiming an equitable interest in Sandalwood Terrace appears insubstantial in relation to the value of the property. The first defendant's estimate of the claimant's interest being worth approximately $10,000 does not seem, on the evidence I have read, a gross underestimate. If, in fact, her interest, once accurately quantified, does turn out to be worth approximately that amount (or even two or three times that amount), by registering a *lis pendens* preventing the property from being sold and by remaining there in exclusive residence for what will probably turn out to be many months, she is taking a stand that seems disproportionate to the probable size of her interest.

On the other hand, the issue of the magnitude of her interest remains in dispute and is a matter to be heard at trial. The application before me did not require a determination of the magnitude of her interest. If it turns out at trial that the magnitude of her interest as calculated by the trial judge is relatively small, it may well be that the trial judge could impose damages for the loss of occupation rent in an amount that exceeds the magnitude of her interest. If she remains in the property, that is the risk she has to accept. Her lawyer's position on this application says to this court that the claimant is aware of this risk and wants to take it.

The first defendant is certainly entitled to occupation rent. No one has argued otherwise. The question for this court is whether or not the court should exercise its discretion and order the claimant to pay a proportion of the occupation rent *now*.

I have decided that this court should not exercise its discretion in favour of the first defendant. I can reasonably infer from the evidence put before me that he is suffering little financial hardship because of his exclusion from the property. In short, he does not need the rent.

Moreover – and this is the more important reason – while I accept counsel's argument that, in certain circumstances, using an interim application to pressure parties into settlement is not improper, this is not an appropriate case for the court to assist in exerting this kind of pressure. The balance of financial power already weighs overwhelmingly in favour of the first defendant, who is obviously being helped directly and indirectly by his father. It also appears from the facts presented that the first defendant heightened the financial pressure on the claimant through the registration of the mortgage – a mortgage that may or may not turn out to be fraudulent, but one that certainly seems to have played a part in provoking the claimant to commence legal action. Now, the first defendant wants this court to assist him further and apply even more financial pressure in a situation that may never have resulted in acrimonious litigation had it not been for the registration of that mortgage.

In this situation, the court should not exercise its discretion in favour of the first defendant. Accordingly, the first defendant's application is dismissed. The first defendant is ordered to pay legal costs to the claimant within 14 days in the amount of $4,000, failing which the first defendant's counterclaim is stayed with liberty to apply or pending further order of this court.

Commentary

This is the most complex case study in this book. It deals not only with a variety of legal and procedural issues in an interim payment application, it also highlights the strategic uses of an interim application. But the objectives of a strategy, as both counsel were aware, need to be consistent with the overriding objective of the Rules (r 1.1), which is to enable the court to deal with cases justly. When launching or continuing legal action, lawyers need to pay attention to this rule. When initiating or defending an interim application, whatever strategy they adopt should be consistent with this rule.

In Wentworth's mind, his strategy on behalf of McKenzie Jr was consistent with the rule. He was just applying a little pressure to get the dispute settled. And, achieving fair settlements, it can be argued, is the overriding objective of the entire civil justice system of which the Rules are a part.

Wentworth did have an arguable case. Because of a peculiarity in the law, Belinda Handsworth was able legally to tie up an expensive piece of property and deprive its owner of using it despite the fact that her claim, when looked at closely, was a small one. Wentworth reasoned that her conduct amounted to legalised oppression and, though the McKenzies had a lot more money than she did, they were still the victims. Wentworth argued that, to put both parties back on a more equal footing and persuade Belinda to settle, she should be made to pay some occupation rent until trial. That was the essence of Wentworth's application.

Wentworth's understanding of the policy behind r 1.1 was sound. When the court pointed out that, contrary to r 1.1, the legal costs of bringing his application seemed disproportionate to the amount he was claiming for occupation rent, he responded positively to the judge's queries. He thanked the judge for bringing him to the 'crux of the whole case', but then turned it on its head as he had promised to do earlier: it was Belinda who was conducting herself in a way that was totally disproportionate to her claim. She was tying up valuable property to secure a very small claim. He went further, focusing on the facts, digging into her affidavit, citing several parts of it to demonstrate how angry she was. He used her own words to show that she was abusing the civil justice system for her own vengeful purposes.

But, in the end, the court was not convinced, and did not grant McKenzie Jr's application. This was a big loss, inasmuch as the court ordered him to pay costs immediately. Whatever momentum the McKenzies felt they could generate by taking the initiative ground to a halt.

One of the reasons Wentworth lost was Temple's counter-strategy. He focused on the facts too – particularly the McKenzies' outsized financial resources and crude attempts at their own brand of oppression. He pointed to exhibit A of Handsworth's affidavit, showing how much money McKenzie Jr was drawing out from Wellington Pipe Ltd, particularly in the last year. He then directed the spotlight on to three large withdrawals from the company that took place shortly after McKenzie Jr was ousted from Sandalwood Terrace. Since the McKenzies were claiming that those withdrawals were loans and not income, Temple's spotlight threw even more suspicion on the already suspicious-looking mortgage granted by McKenzie Jr.

Temple reminded the court in several different ways that it was the McKenzies who had the money and not his client. They were the financial oppressors. The mortgage and interim payment application were proof. Careful to avoid contentiousness, Temple told the court he had not yet proved the mortgage was fraudulent. He succeeded in showing, however, that it was a 'transparently high pressure tactic'. Temple thus used emotional appeal backed up with solid facts to demonstrate why the court should not exercise its discretion in favour of McKenzie Jr.

In retrospect, Wentworth had much to overcome in order to win the application. To an objective observer, the McKenzies did appear to be oppressors and the mortgage did look suspicious. For the court to exercise its discretion in favour of Wentworth's client, it would have had to ignore the mortgage or treat it lightly. It could not do this for the simple reason that Temple, claimant's counsel, used it to prove his theory. His theory was that the defendants were the bullies – the mortgage was proof – and that the judge should not encourage more bullying by granting the order McKenzie Jr was seeking.

The problem with Wentworth's strategy was that he did not consider the whole case in a flexible way. If his client's goal was to apply pressure to Belinda Handsworth to induce her to settle, he should have formulated a completely different strategy. Before initiating the application for interim payment, he should have asked for his client's instructions to negotiate with

Temple to discharge the mortgage. This could have led to the discontinuation of the legal action against all three defendants for fraudulent conveyance. Wentworth could have offered to pay Belinda's legal costs, but without admitting any liability for fraud. By discharging the mortgage and getting the fraudulent conveyance action discontinued, Wentworth could have achieved the following:

- McKenzie Sr and his company, McKenzie Pipe Ltd, would no longer be parties to the legal action. Only Belinda's trust action against McKenzie Jr in relation to Sandalwood Terrace would remain.

- Temple would no longer be able to seek discovery against McKenzie Sr and the company, thus severely limiting the amount of information about McKenzie Jr's finances that Temple would be able to obtain.

- The suspicious-looking mortgage would be gone and Temple would no longer be able to use it against McKenzie Jr.

With the mortgage and McKenzie Sr out of the way, the 'bully factor' could have been greatly reduced and a little more sympathy might have flowed naturally from the judge to McKenzie Jr. Wentworth's argument to obtain an interim payment for occupation rent could then have generated some emotional appeal.

But Wentworth failed to generate any sympathy for his client. This failure grew out of the nature of his relationship with his client. From the very beginning, he failed to take instructions directly from McKenzie Jr. Instead, he took instructions from his father, McKenzie Sr. This inevitably led to Wentworth ignoring his client's real dilemma.

That dilemma stemmed from the nature of the relationships between the three parties, Belinda, McKenzie Jr and McKenzie Sr. The two dominant figures, Belinda and McKenzie Sr, were at loggerheads, struggling to control the weaker figure, McKenzie Jr. Being pulled in opposite directions, Jr was conflicted, timid and indecisive. Although not a psychologist, Wentworth should have seen Jr's difficulty and found a way to address it.

At one point, Wentworth did recommend that he act only for McKenzie Jr and that another lawyer act for McKenzie Sr and the company. But Wentworth's motive was to avoid the appearance of collusion by all three parties against Belinda, not to solve the problem of his acting for two people – father and son – whose interests were potentially in conflict.

As McKenzie Jr's lawyer, his duty was to act solely in Jr's best interest and to solve *his* problem, not McKenzie Sr's. Wentworth failed in this duty. Although he was obviously aware of the issue that he should be taking instructions from McKenzie Jr, by his own admission, he continued to treat McKenzie Sr as his *de facto* client. As he said:

I made it clear that all instructions to me had to come from McKenzie Jr. McKenzie Sr seemed unmoved about this because he would call me at least once a day and try to give me instructions. After protesting several times, I finally insisted that all instructions had to be in writing signed by McKenzie Jr. Nobody seemed concerned about that. McKenzie Sr just laughed it off, getting his secretary to type the instruction letters for McKenzie Jr to sign. It does appear that Jr was not strong enough to stand up to his father. But that was something for Jr to deal with, not me [p 153].

A wise counsel would have drummed up some empathy for his client's predicament. But, Wentworth was unable to do so because he was unclear about who he was acting for. In that confusion, he neglected to feel a sense of loyalty towards Jr. This undermined his ability to understand Jr's problems and to determine what should be done to resolve them.[1] Without that understanding, Wentworth was handicapped in working out an integrated strategy for the case as a whole. It also left him unable to advocate his client's case effectively in the courtroom.

What should Wentworth have done?

He should have invested time in building a trusting relationship with Jr and persuading him to think about his own goals. If McKenzie Jr desired a more conciliatory approach with Belinda, Wentworth could have recommended mediation. If McKenzie Jr expressed a wish to reconcile with Belinda, Wentworth could have suggested counselling. If McKenzie Jr was adamant about continuing the fight with Belinda, Wentworth could have negotiated to get rid of the mortgage and then, possibly, increased the pressure on Belinda with an interim application.

Wentworth did not help Jr identify his goals. It was McKenzie Sr's goals that led to the decisions Wentworth made. McKenzie Sr wanted to exert pressure on Belinda because he wanted Sandalwood Terrace back so he could develop it. Without taking a close look at the options that might benefit McKenzie Jr, Wentworth marched straight ahead with Sr's instructions, exploring and then deciding on the interim payment application. Wentworth thought he was thinking strategically to solve his client's problems, but he was just responding to the person who was paying the bills. Wentworth could not see the forest for the trees. If he had concentrated on solving McKenzie Jr's problem and not his father's, he might have developed a winning solution for his client.

---

1   It could be argued that Wentworth was in breach of his ethical duty to act in the best interests of his client. In the [English] *Guide to the Professional Conduct of Solicitors*, this is referred to as one of the very first ethical duties of the solicitor (Principle 1.01). Ethics and its effect on advocacy is the subject of the next chapter.

CHAPTER 8

ETHICS AND THE QUALITY OF ADVOCACY

In the previous chapter, we saw how Wentworth dealt with a problem that could be characterised as an ethical problem. It was a conflict, or potential conflict, of interest between two clients, McKenzie Jr being Wentworth's actual client and McKenzie Sr his *de facto* client. It can be argued that the conflict of interest between these two clients led not only to an ethical lapse, but also a functional failure. It caused Wentworth to do a less than satisfactory job for McKenzie Jr and it led to poor quality advocacy. But, conflict of interest is just one of many ethical problems that litigation lawyers confront in their day to day practice. In this final chapter, we focus on another ethical problem that litigation lawyers face and which also affects the quality of their advocacy: the conflict between the lawyer's duty to the client and duty to the court. The way lawyers deal with this conflict influences not only their ethical standards, but also their practical effectiveness as advocates.

ETHICAL ADVOCACY AS EFFECTIVE ADVOCACY

Duties to client and court (along with a variety of other ethical duties) have long been codified in Codes of Conduct for lawyers. Every jurisdiction has its own Code of Conduct, some providing more guidance in the practice of law than others. Although the courts are empowered to punish lawyers for breaches of ethical duty, this power is not often exercised. It is usually the professional bodies such as law societies and bar associations that take action against a lawyer who breaches ethical duties. And this does not often occur unless someone files a complaint and the breach is serious.

The Code of Conduct for English solicitors, *The Guide to the Professional Conduct of Solicitors*, contains a rule for litigation lawyers that reflects the tension between the duty to the client and the court. Principle 22.01 reads as follows: 'Solicitors who act in litigation, whilst under a duty to do their best for their client, must never deceive or mislead the court.'[1]

The duty to the client is based on the nature of the lawyer's professional relationship with the client. It is a relationship based on trust. The client trusts the lawyer to use his or her professional skill to uphold the client's best

---

1   The ethical duties referred to in this chapter can be found in *The Guide to the Professional Conduct of Solicitors*, particularly Chapter 22. Readers should note that this book does not contain a thoroughgoing discussion of ethical problems. Readers are advised to refer to Codes of Conduct and other applicable rules in their own jurisdictions.

interests, subject to certain other duties, but to the exclusion of any other interests including the interest of the lawyer. Out of this client-comes-first relationship arise a number of lawyers' sub-duties, for example, the duty to treat client communications as confidential, the duty never to use confidences to their own advantage and, in court, the practical duty to do their best to win.

The duty to the court is based on the lawyer's status as officer of the court. From this flows the duty not to deceive or mislead the court. Lawyers must not make statements they know are false; they must not mislead the court by misstating evidence; they must not permit a witness to give evidence they know is false. Lawyers are also under a duty to inform the court of all relevant law of which they are aware, even if it supports the other side's case.

The tension between duties to client and court arises because of the nature of the adversarial system and the resultant pressure exerted on the lawyer. In the adversarial system, there is intense pressure on lawyers to win for their clients and some have been known to buckle under the pressure, compromising their duty to the court. The reasons they give all too often reveal the weaker side of human nature: 'I did not inform the court because I didn't think it was relevant;' 'My client insisted that I do it that way;' 'My colleagues told me that the approach I was taking was okay;' 'If I had disclosed that information it would have destroyed my case.'

Even when there is only a little pressure, a natural temptation exists for lawyers to make expedient decisions that favour paying clients over their duty to the court. Lawyers need to resist this temptation and learn ways of reconciling their clients' interests with the integrity of the system in which they operate. The trust placed in them by the system and the community demands this of them. In the heat of battle, lawyers can keep watch on their own ethical performance by remembering or referring to their Codes of Conduct and by consulting more experienced lawyers with a reputation for ethical conduct. The principles outlined in the Codes are the buoys to which they can cling in a sea of ethical dilemmas. When lawyers find ethical problems overwhelming, more experienced lawyers can help to rescue them from sinking beneath the waves.

But responding effectively to ethical problems has an important functional, as well as ethical basis: ethical advocacy goes hand in hand with effective advocacy. To illustrate this point, we can draw on some of the advocacy skills discussed earlier in this book. 'Avoiding contentiousness' is the first example (see, for example, above, pp 12, 20). When you avoid contentiousness, you refrain from making statements of fact that cannot be conclusively established from the material before the court. As a matter of technique, counsel should only make statements of fact that are consistent with the material presented. To suggest the existence of facts that are not before the court, or that cannot reasonably be inferred from the material before the court, is to risk provoking the judge to take notice, to disagree with you and possibly to lose trust in your argument. Being careful about how you put the facts before the judge actually trains you to refrain from misstating the facts. Thus, avoiding contentiousness is not only an advocacy skill, it is also an ethical way to practise advocacy.

A second example is the technique of using law appropriately in argument (see above, p 8). When you use law in argument, you have an ethical duty to cite all relevant cases. Failure to do so can undermine the trust judges put in what you say. When you refer to a case, be sure to explain accurately the facts of the case and the court's decision. If the judge detects inaccuracies in your presentation of the facts or in the way you explain the legal principles, this will diminish the persuasiveness of your argument. When you use law appropriately in argument, you are not only practising effective advocacy skills, but also meeting high ethical standards.

A third example of how ethics and advocacy skills coincide can be explained in relation to telling 'an appealing story', one of the four basic elements of effective advocacy discussed in Chapter 1 (see p 3). For a story to be appealing, it should have logical and emotional appeal. But, as Hartje and Wilson explain in their book, *Lawyers' Work*, the story should also have ethical appeal. Ethical appeal comes from the advocate who is telling the story. If that person has high standards of ethical conduct, the story will have ethical appeal. A judge will be more easily persuaded by an advocate with an ethical reputation than one whose trustworthiness is in doubt. This is a strong inducement for lawyers to avoid lapses in conduct and to maintain an ethical reputation throughout their careers.

GREY AREAS OF ETHICAL DECISION MAKING

For those new to legal practice, however, it is not always easy to locate the line between what is honest and what is deceptive in a court of law, especially when there is so much pressure to win. When playing to win, it is only natural that lawyers want to show as little of their hand as they can get away with. But, procedural rules, such as rules relating to discovery, demand they disclose as much of their hand as the other side or the judge can properly demand of them. The result of all this hide and seek is that, while most lawyers abide by most rules, the conduct of many falls close to the line – into grey areas of ethical decision making. A grey area is a decision a lawyer makes, the ethics of which is debatable, but one which is unlikely to result in a sanction imposed by the court or a professional body.

Take the case of *R v Balsam* (case study 2). This is the case of the student found at the airport with a suitcase full of dangerous drugs. Counsel, Ms Calhoun, was doing a bail application on Balsam's behalf. Prior to the application, counsel made a conscious decision not to inform the court that Balsam had a prior conviction for possession of marijuana in another country.

This is not an uncommon situation. The prosecution may not have full details of the defendant's prior convictions at the time of the bail hearing. But defence counsel, having already talked to the client or having acted for the client before, may know all the details. In that situation, the duty of confidentiality owed to the client will prevail and counsel has a positive duty not to reveal the prior conviction without the client's express consent. That is the position Balsam's counsel took.

In many jurisdictions, this would not be considered unethical or improper. It would not amount to deceiving the court, because deceiving the court usually means saying or doing something actively to deceive. If Balsam's lawyer had asserted Balsam had no prior convictions, for example, that assertion would have been actively deceiving the court, but all Balsam's counsel said in that regard was that the *prosecution* was not alleging any prior convictions (see above, p 32).

An ethical issue does arise, however, and it does land Balsam's counsel in a grey area. Counsel did tell the court that Balsam was not known to be involved in criminal activity and that this was one reason why he should be granted bail. Strictly speaking, as far as the police were concerned, this was true. The police did not know that he was involved in criminal activity, but counsel did know. And the remainder of counsel's submission was based on the unspoken premise that her client had never been involved in criminal activity before. Possession of marijuana may not be a serious crime, but no judge would agree that it is not criminal activity. Arguably, then, a kind of deception did occur. Counsel must have thought that, as a practical matter, neither the prosecution nor the court would discover that Balsam told his lawyer about the marijuana conviction. Furthermore, she must have known that what she said was not enough to constitute a flagrant breach of ethical duty. Nevertheless, counsel did stray into a grey area, close to the line, managing to stay on the right side of it only by choosing her words carefully.

CONSEQUENCES OF STRAYING INTO GREY AREAS

Even if counsel does not get caught, straying into grey areas can put both counsel and counsel's case at risk. The fear of getting caught can weaken counsel's confidence. The failure to put forward the case as honestly as one should can sap strength from counsel's arguments. As counsel handles a greater number of cases, the habit of sojourning into grey areas can also nudge counsel ever closer to the line leaving him or her less conscious of when it is being crossed and increasingly vulnerable to exposure and punishment.

This can occur as easily in civil non-trial applications as it can in criminal matters. When lawyers draft affidavits for an interim application, for example, they have a duty not to misstate the facts or participate in misstating them. If a client misstates the facts in an affidavit, the lawyer is under a duty to correct the affidavit if the lawyer knows that the client is misstating the facts. If the client refuses, the lawyer may have no alternative but to insist on being released from the retainer. But, lawyers are not often certain whether their clients are telling the truth. Moreover, in communicating with clients, lawyers do not have a duty to ascertain the truth of what their clients tell them unless what they hear calls for further elaboration or investigation, that is, unless they are 'put on inquiry'. In that case, they have a duty, where practicable, to check the truth of what they are told. But, unlike judges, they need not establish by weighing the evidence that it is the truth.

In case study 5, *Dalton v Wagner*, Otto Wagner's lawyer, Marlene Taylor, was sceptical of Wagner's story that, when he gave Rita Dawn Vigers a cheque for $25,000, it was only a loan. Wagner said he was acting only as Rita's agent in the sale of the car; he did not buy that car from her. After hearing that, Ms Taylor was put on inquiry and she did indeed inquire. She said that she probed her client's story with cross-examination (see above, p 97). Although Wagner's answers did not seem very satisfactory, she did not probe further. She was satisfied only that his story was plausible, so she put it in an affidavit. When Ms Taylor used Otto Wagner's affidavit in court to support his defence of agency, she did not misstate or exaggerate the evidence he included in his affidavit. She did not state that she thought it was true. She merely put it before the court. If her client was misstating the facts, that was his responsibility, not hers. In the adversarial system, establishing the truth is the court's job, not the lawyer's. That is the way the lawyer, Marlene Taylor, viewed her own conduct.

As in Balsam's bail application, Ms Taylor's conduct probably did not cross the line into deception, but it did stray into a grey area. She suspected that what her client was going to swear in an affidavit was false, so she made some perfunctory inquiries and came up with the conclusion that maybe it was not false. She did not go far enough in her inquiries to check the truth of what Wagner was saying. Even so, it is virtually unthinkable that the judge or the Law Society's discipline committee would ever investigate. In the event, the consequence to Ms Taylor was not discipline for unethical conduct. It was simply that she could not argue her case with absolute confidence and her case had serious weaknesses in it. Her opponent, Ms Harrington, spotted the weaknesses in Wagner's affidavit and exploited them in argument. Despite her clever advocacy, Ms Taylor lost.

That loss and her involvement in producing and relying on that sort of affidavit may or may not leave a blemish on her reputation. But, if Ms Taylor is farsighted enough, in future she will refrain from stepping into grey areas such as these. Walking the fine line between truthfulness and deception is never easy to do. For an advocate, it is a high wire act that can lead to a hard fall.

SKILLS AND VIGILANCE IN
THE ADVERSARIAL SYSTEM

Occasionally, we see lawyers who walk the high wire but never seem to fall. They breach their Code of Conduct, but never get caught. This poses an interesting problem for other lawyers: if there are indeed lawyers who do not get caught, how do you protect your clients from these people? Even more fundamental is this question: how do you protect your clients when people – both lawyers and their clients on the opposite side of your dispute – are involved in questionable conduct of any kind? Effective advocacy is not only ethical advocacy; it is also protecting your clients from the lack of ethics in others.

In *Dalton v Wagner*, Ms Harrington solved the problem not just by being skilled, but by being vigilant. To investigate a known swindler like Otto Wagner, she retained an investigator. She prepared thoroughly, focusing relentlessly on the facts. She was able to identify the weaknesses in Wagner's affidavit, showing that Wagner's story was improbable. Although she had information that Wagner was a swindler, she put her case to the court diplomatically so as to avoid contentiousness (see above, pp 104–06). She had achievable goals and a flexible strategy: having obtained an order compelling Wagner to make payment into court, she did not continue chasing him with litigation procedures. She reduced the risks for her client by negotiating a quick end to the dispute.

If lawyers are not sufficiently alert to the potential for deviousness in the other side, the result can be devastating no matter how meritorious their case may be. In case study 6, *The Commonwealth Bank of Metroland v Jonathan and Robert Beaumont*, Mr Weiler, Dr Beaumont's lawyer, deliberately refrained from interviewing Jonathan Beaumont, the doctor's son, and getting an affidavit from him (see above, p 134). Weiler strongly suspected that Jonathan Beaumont's story would hurt his client. By deciding not to interview Jonathan Beaumont, Weiler was not breaching any ethical rules. His decision was not even in a grey area. Except for prosecutors, there is no rule requiring the production of witnesses whose evidence will hurt your case. Nevertheless, he was playing a crafty game that the bank's lawyer, Ms Stolar, seemed unaware of.

In her submission, Ms Stolar made no reference to the absence of an affidavit from Jonathan Beaumont. Jonathan Beaumont was the only other witness to events surrounding the transaction, yet Ms Stolar did not draw the court's attention to the fact that the court had not heard from him. Because she was not sufficiently vigilant, Weiler gained the high ground and defeated her application that, at first, seemed strong on the merits.

In the final analysis, while it is essential to build a reputation for ethical conduct, advocates must accept that, in the adversarial system, the opposition

– lawyers and parties alike – do not have good intentions toward them. Lawyers need to be alert to the fact that the other side's intent is to defeat them. When you are in the middle of litigation, it is invariably safest to assume that your adversaries, like you, are thinking strategically and are able to carry out what they have planned. How they behave in the process may come out at either end of the ethical spectrum, or it may fall into the grey areas of human conduct. When going to court, advocates need to be prepared to detect and handle all manner of human weakness. For lawyers to assume that everyone is trustworthy is to risk compromising their most important ethical duty – the duty to clients skilfully to uphold their best interests. At the courtroom door, the watchword is vigilance. The hope is that this book will help you to develop the skills and the vigilance you need to help your clients win the justice they deserve.

BIBLIOGRAPHY

Bevitt, A and Stanton, L, *Criminal Advocacy: A Practical Guide*, 1997, London: Cavendish Publishing

Binder, DA and Bergman, P, *Fact Investigation: From Hypothesis To Proof*, 1984, St Paul, Minn: West

Boon, A, *Advocacy*, 2nd edn, 1999, London: Cavendish Publishing

Brown, B (ed), *Chambers Practice*, 1993, Vancouver, BC: Continuing Legal Education Society of British Columbia

Dessem, RL, *Pretrial Litigation: Law, Policy and Practice*, 2nd edn, 1996, St Paul, Minn: West

Evans, K, *The Golden Rules of Advocacy*, 1993, London: Blackstone

Evans, K, *The Language of Advocacy*, 1998, London: Blackstone

Foster, C, Bourne, C, Gilliat, J and Popat, P, *Civil Advocacy: A Practical Guide*, 2nd edn, 2001, London: Cavendish Publishing

Hartje, JH and Wilson, ME, *Lawyers' Work*, 1984, Seattle: Butterworths

Haydock, RS, Herr, DF and Stempel, JW, *Fundamentals of Pre-Trial Litigation*, 3rd edn, 1994, St Paul, Minn: West

Hendriks, MR, *Court Motions Handbook*, 1991, Toronto: Carswell

Hyam, M, *Advocacy Skills*, 4th edn, 1999, London: Blackstone

Inns of Court School of Law, *Advocacy*, 3rd edn, 1998, London: Blackstone

Manes, RD, *Organized Advocacy: A Manual for the Litigation Practitioner*, 1983, Toronto: Carswell

Mauet, TA, *Pretrial*, 3rd edn, 1995, Boston: Aspen Law and Business

May, A (LJ) (ed), *Civil Procedure (The White Book Service 2000)* 2000, London: Sweet & Maxwell

Napley, D (Sir), *The Technique of Persuasion*, 4th edn, 1991, London: Sweet & Maxwell

Nathanson, S, *What Lawyers Do: A Problem-Solving Approach to Legal Practice*, 1997, London: Sweet & Maxwell

O'Hare, J, Browne, K and Hill, R, *Civil Litigation*, 9th edn, 2000, London: Sweet & Maxwell

Plant, C (ed), *Blackstone's Civil Practice 2000*, London: Blackstone

Re, ED, *Brief Writing and Oral Argument*, 6th edn, 1987, Dobbs Ferry, NY: Oceana

Shields, JD (ed), *Mastering Civil Chambers*, 1997, Vancouver, BC: Continuing Legal Education Society of British Columbia

Sime, S, *A Practical Approach to Civil Procedure*, 4th edn, 2000, London: Blackstone

Speiser, SM, *Lawsuit*, 1980, New York: Horizon

Taylor, N (ed), *Guide to the Professional Conduct of Solicitors*, 6th edn, 1993, London: The Law Society

INDEX